CREATING AND MANAGING an Association Government Relations Program

EDITED BY
Michael E. Kastner

An ASAE Government Relations Section Project

asae

American Society of Association Executives
WASHINGTON, D.C.

Information in this book is accurate as of the time of publication and consistent with standards of good practice in the general management community. As research and practice advance, however, standards may change. For this reason, it is recommended that readers evaluate the applicability of any recommendation in light of particular situations and changing standards.

American Society of Association Executives
1575 I Street, NW
Washington, DC 20005
Phone: (202) 626-2723
Fax: (202) 408-9634
E-mail: books@asae.asaenet.org

George Moffat, Publisher
Linda Munday, Director of Book Publishing
Trish Thomas, Book Acquisitions Coordinator
Zachary Dorsey, Production Coordinator

Cover and interior design by Troy Scott Parker, Cimarron Design

LIBRARY OF CONGRESS CATALOGING-IN-PUBLICATION DATA

Creating and managing an association government relations program /
   Michael E. Kastner, ed.
      p.   cm.
   ISBN 0-88034-140-8. — ISBN 0-88034-141-6 (pbk.)
   1. Trade associations—United States—Management.
   2. Lobbying—United States. I. Kastner, Michael E., 1961-   .
HD2425.A864   1998
060'.68'8—dc21   98-6762
                                                       CIP

Printed in the United States of America

This book is available at a special discount when ordered in bulk quantities. For information, contact ASAE Member Services at (202) 371-0940.

A complete catalog of titles is available on the ASAE home page at http://www.asaenet.org

CONTENTS

FOREWORD

In the United States, our federal government is considered to be a republic democracy, where leaders are elected to represent the interests of the people. One person is sent to Washington to represent the views of many. That person relies on his or her knowledge and wisdom to cast votes on an infinite variety of subjects that concern his or her constituents.

Associations play an integral role in this process. No one person can be an expert on every topic. Fortunately, legislators come from a wide range of professions. Add to that knowledge base professional staffers with even broader areas of expertise, and you have a strong foundation on which to build the decision-making process, but it's still not enough for thorough deliberations on all topics. Congress needs experts from the real world to inform and educate its members so they are able to consider information from all sides of an issue and make the best possible decisions on behalf of constituents. Associations are often the best source for this necessary level of expertise.

Associations act as conduits of information by communicating to their members what Congress is doing in areas that concern them and getting their feedback. Associations can use their government relations efforts to educate members of Congress and their staffs in great detail on how given legislative proposals will affect association members.

Association lobbyists can be likened to bees who carry pollen from one flower to another. Without associations and lobbyists, the system would not be able to function properly. Lobbying on behalf of association members is an appropriate and valuable exercise of the First Amendment right to petition the government for redress of grievances.

Associations can provide Congress with insights not otherwise available on public policy issues. As such, associations should be encouraged to participate in the formation of public policy. Some have called this participation "lobbying by special interests." Well, your association's interests are special, as are the interests of all the others who may be involved in an issue. Every person in this country is represented by one or more special interest groups, whether or not they realize it. I encourage associations to participate in the political process. Association government relations efforts are important and help to make our form of government work.

— *Former Congressman*
Bill Clinger (R-Pa.)

Government Relations in the Association Environment

E. Colette Nelson

MANY ASSOCIATIONS are charged with the mission of ensuring their members' interests are represented before governments in all branches at all levels. For many associations, this means establishing and maintaining relations with the government through direct lobbying, as well as through political action and education.

Lobbying is the art of persuading government policy makers to take a desired action. Lobbying is not a mysterious process. Nor is it immoral. In fact, the right to let your elected officials know how you feel about an issue is embodied in the United States Constitution.

Why should your association get involved in government relations or lobbying? The answer to this question is simple: Your association and its members already are. Whoever your association represents, wherever they are located, your association and its members are affected by hundreds, even thousands, of laws and regulations. Most of these are so routine and so familiar that we hardly notice them at all. Stop signs, parking meters, postage stamps, and speed limits represent laws or regulations we expect and accept.

Frequently, laws that can dramatically affect your association and its members are passed: laws that protect your members from unfair competition; laws that require your members to educate their employees; and laws that require your members to meet minimum standards or obtain a license. These are just a few of the hundreds of laws that tell your members how they will operate on a day-to-day basis.

Believe It or Not, You're in Government Relations

Many associations, including local, regional, and national associations, claim to have no interest in lobbying because they do not pursue government relations activities. But if they looked at their activities more closely, they would see that they already are involved in government relations. The association that invites a government official to its annual awards banquet is in government relations. The association that tracks any legislation or regulations for its members is in government relations. The association whose president is an old school chum of the governor is in government relations. The question is, does your association capitalize on your government contacts?

E. Colette Nelson

If you don't, you are forgoing one of the best opportunities to serve your members. The association structure is uniquely suited to pursuing government relations on behalf of its members. An association is an affinity group—an organization that exists because its members have some interest or interests in common. When those interests might be affected by government at any level, the association is ideally constituted to represent, protect, or enhance those interests before government officials. If members were left to do this individually, few would have sufficient time or expertise to do an adequate job of it, and the cacophony of voices of all members would ensure that no single member carried sufficient weight to achieve what he or she wants from government.

An association also can afford to be "out front," representing the collective opinion of its members on issues that might be too controversial or seemingly too self-serving to be put forward by a single individual or company.

Identifying Issues

If you plan to pursue an agenda in the next legislative session, your association should be doing a lot of work now. You should be determining what issues you want to pursue, what resources can be devoted to pursuing that issue, and what basic research needs to be done to support your case.

One of the most difficult tasks in government relations is identifying the issues to which your association should be devoting its resources. The first step in this process is issue identification. Your association's staff and volunteer leaders should make a habit of listening to your members. Most people spend a lot of time talking about issues that are important to them, whether it's at a cocktail reception, during a casual phone call, or at your government relations committee meeting. Pay attention to what your members are talking about; then figure out if there is something the government can (or should not) do to make your members' lives easier.

Another way to find out what issues are important to your members is to conduct a survey. The American Subcontractors Association (ASA), Alexandria, Va., conducts two annual issues surveys: one of the members of its grassroots network, the other of the government relations chairs of its state and local chapters. ASA's Government Relations Committee uses the results of these surveys to set priorities for the coming year. Because the surveys are conducted annually, ASA also uses them to identify emerging issues.

Some associations retain professional public relations firms to do media tracking. However, you can implement a simple media tracking program yourself. Regularly scan a selection of newspapers and magazines for articles about your industry. Classify the topics of the articles into categories. For example, ASA chapters look for articles on construction safety/accidents, development/environmental issues, and construction workers, among others. An ASA chapter executive director who begins to see a lot of articles about the environment and the quality of life usually can expect to see "no growth" or "slow growth" issues emerge in the next legislative session.

Establishing Policy

It is not enough for association staff to recognize current and emerging issues that may affect members. The association needs to be ready to address these issues in a timely manner. This means educating members about the issues and the effect these issues may have on their day-to-day operations. It also means guiding the association through a consensus-building process toward a policy on the issue.

This process usually entails education of the general membership, perhaps through a series of articles in the association newsletter; discussion at the committee level, including the development of recommended policy; and ultimately, board action on the recommended policy. Staff often must serve as both director of research and facilitator during this policy development process.

Identifying Your Resources

Before deciding what issues the association will tackle, association staff must have a clear understanding of the resources available for a government relations effort. Basic association resources are time and money. However, other resources can contribute to the ultimate success of your government relations program. These include:

- the members and their level of knowledge;
- the leaders and their level of commitment;
- the availability of information on the issue and the time and tools to collect more;
- the availability of professional assistance (e.g., accountants, attorneys) with the skill and commitment to help your efforts;
- the reputation of the association, including its clout, identity, and level of visibility; and
- the reputation of prospective allies, their willingness to help, and the resources available to them.

Setting Priorities: Things to Consider

Once you have identified your association's issues and developed a clear picture of the resources available to your government relations program, you are ready to begin the priority-setting process. There are at least five questions you should ask:

1. **Who are you?** That is, why does the association exist? What is the driving force causing you to act? Review your association's mission statement. This will allow you to determine how important the issue is to your members—ask your members.

2. **How committed is your association?** Conduct a candid evaluation of your association's limits. Do your members understand the issue and why it is important to them? Do they agree that the purpose is worthwhile? Do your leaders and members have the skill and knowledge necessary to carry out their end of the bargain? Do they believe they can influence the government's decision-making process? If the answer to any of these questions is no, you may want to devote your association's resources to something else.

3. **Who is the opposition?** How strong are they? How important is this issue to them? Your association might want to reduce its level of involvement if you're reasonably sure that no sub-

stantial counter effort will be launched. In addition, you'll want to evaluate the effect your activities on this issue will have on your ability to work with the opposing group on another issue, if necessary.

4. **Will your success on the issue have other effects?** Is there someone else or some other group that will be even peripherally affected, either positively or negatively, by your issue? If so, you should consider contacting them to determine their likely level of interest and involvement. Your association may want to reevaluate its level of involvement if other organizations plan a major effort to achieve the outcome your association favors. Caution is advisable, however. A surprise campaign by the other side could develop almost overnight, and you don't want to learn that every group on your side of the issue decided to let all the other groups take the lead.

5. **How right are you?** Although it is not the role of association staff to determine whether the association's position is "right" or "wrong," staff and the association's leaders must have a clear understanding of the opposition's position and the reasons for it. You should have a clear picture of how the association's policy meshes with current social and cultural mores. These, too, may determine how or even whether your association pursues an issue.

Setting Priorities: A Formal Process

The basic steps for setting priorities in the government relations function are as follows:

- Identify problems of your members and different solutions to these problems. Identify issues affecting your members that may be considered by government at any level during the coming year.
- List these issues in order of their overall importance to the association's members. See Table 1-1.

Table 1-1. **Issues in Order of Importance**

1. Daffodil to be state flower.
2. Mountain lion to be state animal.
3. Waltz to be state dance.
4. Trout to be state fish.
5. *War and Peace* to be state book.

- List these same issues in order of their likelihood of being considered by a government body during the coming year or in order of their likelihood of success. Some issues near the top of the list in importance to members may be years from consideration by any government body. See Table 1-2.

Table 1-2. **Issues in Order of "Passability"**

1. Trout to be state fish.
2. Daffodil to be state flower.
3. Mountain lion to be state animal.
4. Waltz to be state dance.
5. *War and Peace* to be state book.

- Combine the importance list and the immediacy list, using a weighted average, to get a single list of issues arranged according to their priority for allocation of association resources. See Table 1-3.

Table 1-3. **Issues in Priority Order**

1. Daffodil to be state flower.	$1 + 2 / 2 = $ **1.5**
2. Lion to be state animal.	$2 + 3 / 2 = $ **2.5**
3. Trout to be state fish.	$4 + 1 / 2 = $ **2.5**
4. Waltz to be state dance.	$3 + 4 / 2 = $ **3.5**
5. *War and Peace* to be state book.	$5 + 5 / 2 = $ **5.0**

Setting Priorities: A Decision-making Tool

Once you have identified issues and listed them in order of importance, other issues will still need to be considered before you decide what level of resources will be devoted to each issue. ASA uses the outline in Table 1-4 to facilitate discussion on whether to get involved in an issue and how aggressive to be in pursuing an issue.

Table 1-4. **A Decision-making Tool**

Use "force" when...	• the issue is very important • you're right • there is something else to be gained • you have the facts to back you up • the cost of losing is high
Compromise when...	• the issue is more important to the other side • there are rights and wrongs on both sides • you're going to have to work with that group in the future (and your actions will make a difference)
Withdraw when...	• the issue is not important • you're wrong • there's more to lose than to gain • you can't win • the time is not right
Wait when...	• you don't have the facts • the time is not right

Phases of Government Relations Involvement

Finally, your association is ready to determine what resources and actions ideally would be employed to deal with each issue. Measure your ideal allocation of resources against what is realistic. Regardless of the size and budget of your association, the ideal will have to be scaled back to fit what you have to work with. (If you don't have to scale back, you are not setting your sights high enough.)

Some issues may be most effectively addressed with an all-out campaign that includes grassroots lobbying and mass visits by members with legislators. Other issues might be best handled through existing or potential coalitions. The following phases of government relations involvement should be considered during planning:

- **Information only.** The staff or a designated member will monitor the issue and report on action taken on it at board meetings, in the association newsletter, or through another established means.

- **Ceremonial presence.** The association will monitor an issue and will participate to a limited extent in opportunities for stating its position. Limited participation might include signing a letter or advertisement prepared by a coalition group or sending a letter for or against proposed legislation. You also may take advantage of every opportunity to promote your association's involvement in the issue to your members. This may include attending meetings or rallies on the issue, seeking out photo opportunities, and ultimately, attending the bill-signing ceremony.

- **Substantive lobbying.** The association will monitor an issue and will actively seek opportunities for formally and informally putting the association's position before legislators or regulators. This probably will include "walking the halls"; that is, your staff, retained lobbyist, and/or members will visit with legislators and their staffs to educate them about the issue and your position. In addition, an association representative may be involved in drafting legislation, analyzing content to determine precise effects on members and the general public, and tracking probable voting on legislation with an eye toward identifying uncommitted votes.

- **Constituent contacts.** Grassroots contacts are one of the most important and effective ways to bolster the effectiveness of your lobbying efforts. A grassroots effort may be as simple as urging your members in the association newsletter to write their legislators or as sophisticated as a "direct dial" campaign in which you call and then link your members directly to their legislators' offices. To increase the effectiveness of your grassroots campaign, you may want to prepare district-by-district analyses of how the issue affects your members. Finally, you should make sure your members learn the outcome of their efforts.

- **Media relations.** The media present still another opportunity to educate the public and, indirectly, government decision makers about your issue. You will want to target your message carefully and deliver your message effectively.

- **Political action.** This last phase of government relations involves convincing your members to "put their money where their mouths are." The association should urge members to contribute to political candidates most likely to support their views. The association may want to form and support its own political action committee.

On any given issue, the association may choose one or more phases of government relations involvement to win. Occasionally, an issue will arise on which your association will want to make a "full-court press." In a full-court press, your association will devote whatever time and resources it can make available to the issue.

CHAPTER 2

Issue Development: A Strategic Marketing Approach

E. Colette Nelson and Michael P. O'Brien, CAE

YOUR SMALL ASSOCIATION may become embroiled in a tax issue that has escalated from a local issue to a statewide debate. Or perhaps you are the new chief executive officer or government relations director and need a strategy to help you learn the art of lobbying. Whatever your issue or agenda, you must persuade your state (or federal) policy makers to take a particular action—that's all lobbying is.

Whether you plan to tackle a single issue or map out a full scheme of association legislative policy, one way to ensure success while using your association's limited resources to best advantage is to treat your lobbying campaign as a marketing campaign. A successful lobbying campaign involves the same type of planning, preparation, and implementation as a campaign to take any sort of product to market. This chapter covers the fundamental steps involved in developing a marketing plan for your association's lobbying agenda.

Identifying the Issue

The first step in any marketing plan is to identify the product or service you want to sell. Identification is the first step with a lobbying campaign as well, but the goal is to sell your solution to a pending issue rather than to sell a product. At first glance, identifying the issue may seem simple. After all, the members of your association are surrounded by problems that need solving. That, in fact, is your problem. There are too many problems to solve and not enough resources to go around.

To conduct a successful lobbying campaign, you must focus resources on the issue or issues that are most important to your members. Scattering the association's efforts will reduce the likelihood of success on any one issue. For example, if a bill to require state licensing of your members' businesses is your highest priority, why spend your association's limited resources on other issues, such as an increase in sales tax, workers' compensation reform, or an official all-industry day?

How do you determine which issue is most important to members? Ask them, and listen to what they have to say. At every meeting and social event, members talk to each other about the problems they are facing. Listen to your members carefully and ask them which issues are most pressing, why, and what ideas they have for solving them.

You also can take the more formal approach of conducting a survey. The American Subcontractors Association (ASA), Alexandria, Va., conducts an annual issues survey to determine member priorities. ASA's Government Relations Committee reviews survey results and recommends legislative priorities to the board for the next year.

In addition to determining the highest priority issue, you also should estimate its chances of success. Don't waste association resources on an issue you have no chance of winning.

ASA's criteria include the following:

- the degree of member commitment—if members won't write letters, the issue isn't important to them;
- whether ASA staff and members have the skill and knowledge to carry out the plan;
- the strength and skill of any allies and of the opposition; and
- the general political climate.

Your lobbyist or a politically savvy member can help you evaluate your situation candidly.

Study the Issue's History

Before you launch a lobbying campaign, you should know the history of your issue. Has it been studied or debated in previous years? If so, what happened? Which legislators supported or opposed the issue? Are they still around? Which individuals and other organized interests were involved?

E. Colette Nelson
and
Michael P. O'Brien,
CAE

Has another state or region addressed the issue? Did similar legislation pass, and was its implementation successful? Which public interest groups were involved with its passage?

You already may have many answers if you've been following your issue for some time. In general, though, the public library is a great resource, especially if it indexes a major newspaper in your state.

Every legislative body has an agency devoted to research. Start your search for information there. If the agency does not have an appropriate expert on staff, ask it to direct you to one.

If you're affiliated with a national association, that may be the best place to start. Your national association may be able to tell you what has and hasn't worked in other states and can put you in contact with members in other states who have lobbied on the same issue. National associations of state legislators—such as the National Conference of State Legislators, Denver, Colorado, and the American Legislative Exchange Council, Washington, D.C., also may be able to help you find out what action other states have taken on your issue.

Gather Information

Getting the history is just one step. You also need to research any technical aspects and related arguments, pro and con. Compile the data that prove your case on the issue.

Information is key. "The way to win in Washington is to present interesting anecdotes backed up with sound statistics," says one association lobbyist. It works at the state and local levels, too. Two principal ingredients in the lobbying campaign information portfolio are statistics and anecdotes.

Statistics are data appropriately organized to present significant information about your issue. You may be able to compile your statistics from existing public information. Alternatively, you may have to conduct or commission a survey. The statistics you gather should describe the problem and show whether or not your proposal offers a solution.

An anecdote is a short, entertaining account of some event, usually personal. Make a point of collecting these stories from members. For the sake of credibility, maintain a system for identifying, verifying, and tracking anecdotes. A simple notebook or computer file can be organized by legislative district. Use this information to illustrate the problem you are trying to solve and to add a human dimension to your presentation.

For example, at ASA one of the key issues is ensuring that state prompt-payment laws cover construction subcontractors. Before initiating a legislative campaign in a state, the association routinely surveys payment practices. The survey results demonstrate whether slow pay is a problem, the extent of the problem, the harm it does to subcontractors, and the harm it does to the government owner. ASA also tracks incidents of slow payment and writes short case studies on how this situation affects the subcontracting firm involved. The case studies are compiled by legislative district, and they are made available to legislators and the media.

E. Colette Nelson
and
Michael P. O'Brien,
CAE

Determine Your Markets

Once you have identified your issue and researched its history, it is time to determine to whom you must sell your position; that is, it's time to determine your markets. Your most obvious buyers are the policy makers whose decisions you want to influence. Find out who they are, and research their political backgrounds and voting records on issues similar to yours. What issues are important to these key policy makers, and what or who influences their decisions?

Where can you get this information? At the federal level, dozens of books describe the background of each member of Congress. At the state level, the secretary of state can provide much of it. Also consider contacting the library and organizations like the League of Women Voters, the Chamber of Commerce, and others. You also may want to seek information from anyone you know who deals with legislators, such as lobbyists and legislative staff members.

The information you gather about the key decision makers on your issue will help you pinpoint other markets. If your legislator toes the party line, you may want to work through party leaders. If he or she craves media coverage, arrange for press recognition of his or her stand on your issue.

If a legislator has close ties with another public interest group, try to get his or her attention through a member of that group. You might even recruit that group to join the coalition supporting your issue.

Develop Sales Tools

Your issue is meaningless without a way to communicate the association's position to identified markets. You need sales tools.

If your issue involves an association initiative, the primary tool is a bill or amendment for which you will seek a legislative sponsor. Bill language should be simple and straightforward. Unfortunately, that is not always possible, particularly when amending an existing statute.

Too many associations begin and end marketing material development with their written bill. Whether you pursue your own initiative or try to defeat someone else's, other tools to develop include a concise one- or two-page fact sheet and a section-by-section analysis of the legislation.

Depending on available resources, consider developing:

- a media kit;
- a pamphlet that makes your association's case using statistics you develop;
- case studies using anecdotes you compile; and
- a videotape discussing the problem and your proposed solution.

Use these materials to inform legislators, potential allies, and the public of your existence and position.

Test Market Your Product

Depending on the complexity of the issue and the extent of your resources, the first steps may take a few weeks or even a year or more. Once you have identified the issue and developed (or at least planned to develop) marketing tools, it is time to test market your product. It is important to talk to potential coalition members and likely legislative sponsors.

Keep in mind that it's often difficult to foresee every impact a proposed bill may have. For example, ASA's Florida chapter discovered recently that language drafted for legislation to ensure prompt payment would have almost the opposite effect.

Have representatives of each of your markets review the association's proposed bill and supporting materials. Be sure that they not only support your objectives, but that they also do not unintentionally harm any other group. Otherwise, you might end up with unexpected opposition.

Every interest group you approach will have a different perspective on the issue. Consider each suggestion. Will it solve the issue you are trying to address while making your bill more passable? If so, modify your bill and supporting materials. If you think it won't, explain your reasoning and try to persuade the group to work with you nonetheless. At ASA, a proposed bill is test marketed a second time if feedback results in major changes. In any event, don't develop too much pride in authorship.

Develop a Sales Plan

The test marketing process also will give you an idea about how public or private the association's sales efforts should be. If your issue is controversial, very limited in scope, or might have negative consequences for another group, consider keeping a low profile. Don't send out news releases or publish stories in your newsletter. Consider asking your legislative sponsor whether it's possible to add your piece to another bill and to press for speedy passage.

Lobbying is personal. All your research and preparation comes down to conversations among you, your lobbyist, your members, and legislators interested in your issue.

E. Colette Nelson
and
Michael P. O'Brien,
CAE

14

Train Your Sales Team

The final ingredient in your marketing plan is your membership. "Grassroots" is more than a buzzword in today's competitive political arena. It is a necessity. High-speed, high-tech communication systems have shown that constituents' opinions really matter.

It doesn't matter how much constituent support and interest you have unless you can prove it. That's where a grassroots network comes in. It is the association's job to educate members about the issue and what the association is doing about it. Don't assume that because the association's government relations committee or board of directors selected the issue and helped develop the lobbying plan, the rest of the association's members are committed to its implementation. You must create interest and build commitment by telling people why they should care and how they can help.

If you merely talk about your issue or throw it on the legislative table, you're almost certain to lose. If you carefully prepare and implement your marketing campaign and manage to avoid the pitfalls of the legislative process, you'll win more than your share of legislative battles.

Lobbying Rules of the Road

With a marketing plan and sales team in place, you're ready to go. Here are some fundamental rules to help you avoid common pitfalls of lobbying:

1. **Never tell a legislator you're smarter than he or she is.**
   It's quite likely that a legislator is not as informed on the issue as

you are. Your job is to educate the legislator in a forthright manner. Don't orate, lecture, or preach.

2. **Develop your program in advance.** If you can anticipate a problem and start talking about it right away, you can define and limit the legislative debate. That's what your marketing plan is all about.

3. **Don't get divided—there is strength in unity.** This is one of many reasons it's important to keep your members informed about the issue and what you are doing about it. This also is the reason to be careful about whom you invite to participate in your coalition.

4. **Lobby at home.** Going to the state capital can be important, but the most effective lobbying is done in the legislator's home district. Visit legislators in their home town.

5. **Get other people and groups involved.** This is the era of coalitions. Find out who else your issue might affect and get them involved.

6. **Trust your lobbyist.** Your lobbyist must have the flexibility to negotiate during the push and tug of the legislative process. Make sure he or she knows in advance which parts of your proposal you can concede and which you can't. Don't tie the lobbyist's hands too tightly, though.

7. **Keep informed.** The legislative process frequently moves very quickly, particularly at the state and local levels. It's sometimes nearly impossible to keep up with amendments, refinements, compromises, and so on. Make sure you check with your lobbyist before you write a legislative update or visit a legislator.

8. **Stroke your legislators.** Remember that legislators almost always want to be reelected. It's important to them to be recognized for their efforts. Give awards, hold thank-you receptions, mention them in articles, have them write for you, and invite them to speak to your association. Check the lobbying and disclosure laws that apply before you present a gift or reimburse a legislator for services such as a speech.

CHAPTER 3

Managing and Staffing a Government Affairs Committee

Michael P. O'Brien, CAE, and E. Colette Nelson

THE ASSOCIATION COMMITTEE STRUCTURE is the key to fulfilling the mission of any association. In a member-driven association, committees are where members make the decisions that guide staff actions and determine how resources are spent. Each association committee is an important component of the association, and many of the group dynamics of committees are the same, regardless of committee type (for example, communications, education, finance, and so forth).

Committees that function well act as the catalyst that allows the association to meet the needs and advance the goals of its members. However, poor management of association committees also can lead the association into a morass of stagnation and eternal strife. As comedian Fred Allen once mused, "A committee is a gathering of important people who singly can do nothing, but together can decide that nothing can be done."

Although government affairs or legislative committees share many of the same characteristics of other committees, they pose special problems for association staff responsible for them. The intricate world of federal, state, and local politics in which an association government affairs committee must operate often poses unique problems and circumstances for members and staff alike.

The Role of Government Affairs Committees

The basic mission of any government affairs committee is to recommend policy to the association on legislative, regulatory, and legal issues. The committee is responsible for analyzing issues, addressing technical components, and educating the membership about how legislation, regulations, and court decisions will affect the industry. The government affairs committee, sometimes in conjunction with the board of directors, also is responsible for setting legislative priorities, devising strategy, and allocating time and resources.

Many association staff liaisons have discovered that the political environment of a government affairs committee often can rival the political jungle of the government to which it is supposed to respond. Association staff encounter many of the same problems in a government affairs committee as any other committee, such as apathy, bickering, regionalism, stalemates, personality clashes, indecisiveness, grandstanding, and so forth. The committee structure itself is inherently political because many associate members view committees as their way to influence their industry or as a vehicle to fulfill their own agenda and leadership aspirations. These problems tend to be magnified in direct relation to the importance the association places on government relations. The higher the profile of the government affairs committee, the more risk it runs of becoming an ineffective tool for setting association legislative policy and priorities.

In addition to the universal aspects of committee management, government affairs committees (and its staff) also are at the mercy of committee members' individual political views, convictions, and sometimes, prejudices. A government affairs committee must achieve its mission while contending with a complex set of factors on which it has little or no influence. Those factors include party politics, the economy, government bureaucracies, industry rivals, organized opposition, competing issues, and the media.

Despite this veritable minefield of problems, many associations have established effective government affairs committees that meet the needs and advance the goals of their respective members. This success often can be attributed to chairs, committee members, and staff who understood their roles—and each other's.

Michael P. O'Brien,
CAE, and
E. Colette Nelson

18

The Role of the Committee Chair

The body of literature on the role of committee chairs in general is extensive. A concise description of the chair's role can be found in the U.S. Chamber of Commerce's *Guide to Association Committees* (1987), which divides a chair's duties into five categories:

1. Planning
2. Conducting meetings
3. Maintaining records and information
4. Getting action
5. Evaluating results

Desirable Traits in a Chair

The *Guide to Association Committees* provides a checklist to guide the selection of committee chairs. The chair should have:

- the ability to communicate;
- a record of participation and interest in the association's activities;
- a willingness to listen;
- the ability to command attention and to inspire leaders;
- the ability to control without domination;
- knowledge of parliamentary procedure;
- initiative;
- prestige and respect within the industry;
- an understanding of the power relationship within and among committees;
- knowledge of the subject area in which the committee functions;
- the ability to think and act in terms of the association's overall goals and objectives;
- the ability to create the right atmosphere for productive committee work;
- the availability to carry out responsibilities; and
- a clear understanding of the position of association staff and the need for a close working relationship.

A chair who has all these traits comes along only rarely in the career of an association executive. Those chairs are fondly, and often wistfully, remembered by staff and usually qualify for the "Chair Made in Association Heaven Award." Just looking at the list of desirable traits makes one realize that a combination of only some of these traits in the wrong person can spell disaster (for example, a chair who has initiative, understands parliamentary procedure, and has prestige within the industry but does not understand the subject area, does not listen, is never available, and cannot work with staff).

Selection of the Chair

Assuming that the government affairs committee is a high-profile committee of the association, the chair of this committee must be able to comfortably operate in the often conflicting world of association and government politics. In most associations, committee chairs are chosen by the elected president. This fact of association life often determines whether the staff's life during the chair's tenure will be bearable or not. The importance, therefore, that the president places on government relations will help to determine whom he or she selects to chair the government affairs committee.

Michael P. O'Brien, CAE, and E. Colette Nelson

Working with Staff

As with other committees, the chair's ability to properly manage meetings is often the key to success for a government affairs committee. Although it is usually safe to assume that your committee chair is politically ambitious within the association, it is important that he or she not have an external political agenda. In other words, this person's main goal as chair should not be to address only his or her own legislative issues or political causes. It also is sometimes difficult for a government affairs committee chair to look at issues as they affect the whole membership and not just himself or herself. Very often it may fall to staff to demonstrate the true effect of an issue on the industry. A common example of this is when the committee chair owns a large business in an industry composed primarily of small businesses. An issue of tremendous concern to small business members may be only a minor matter to the chair. If the chair still fails to see the importance of the issue, it may be wise to have a committee member speak to the chair on the importance of the issue.

The committee chair should be able to see and understand political realities. Once a chair is appointed, staff should ensure that he or she is briefed completely on the political situation of the federal, state, or local government, depending on the scope of the committee's jurisdiction.

Although it is not a problem for the chair to be a member of one political party or the other, the chair must not look at all issues as either Democratic or Republican. Most associations must deal with both parties on different issues. The party composition of the city council, the state legislature, and the U.S. Congress often will dictate, in part, how strategy on different issues is determined. A chair who thinks that all Democrats are evil and that the association should not support any Democratic initiatives will be in for a rude awakening if Democrats control the bodies of government.

Just as they may not see how an issue fails to affect certain portions of the membership, government affairs committee chairs often fail to see how an issue affects other areas. Frequently, an issue that affects one portion of the country may not have reached, and may never reach, the hometown or state of the chair. In these situations, the chair may need to be sensitized to the issue by staff and committee members.

The opposite is true when the chair's hometown may have dealt with an issue long ago that is now affecting other areas in the association jurisdiction. Although the chair may offer valuable insight on the issue, he or she may have lost enthusiasm for tackling an issue that is no longer of personal concern. The chair may need to realize that the methods he or she used to approach the issue five or ten years ago may no longer be appropriate and effective.

Although it is rare for staff to have to contend with a government affairs committee chair who suffers from all of the above flaws, staff will, in the course of an association career, probably eventually encounter all of them because none are uncommon. Even with these flaws, a chair who can run a good meeting and support the decisions of the committee before the board of directors will accomplish the basic mission of the committee.

The Role of Committee Members

Desirable Traits in Committee Members

There also is quite a bit of literature on the role of committee members in the association committee structure. The American Society of Association Executives' *Getting Involved: The Challenge of Committee Participation* (1990) offers a concise list of the qualities desirable in committee members:

1. They are either knowledgeable about or interested in the committee's area of activity.
2. They know who the committee chair is.
3. They know what the specific responsibilities of the committee are.
4. They know what the association's practices, policies, and procedures are.

5. They know what the responsibilities of the association staff to the committee are.
6. They know what the past performance of the committee has been.
7. They know what the reporting procedure to the board of directors is.
8. They establish realistic, attainable goals.
9. They give recognition to the committee chair and other members of the committee.
10. They get involved and participate.

Michael P. O'Brien, CAE, and E. Colette Nelson

Few committee members will have all these desirable traits. If the chief elected officer is making the appointments, association politics may dictate additional qualifications for appointment. Because government affairs committees usually are high profile, appointment to them often is viewed as more desirable than appointment to other, less prominent committees. Therefore, the government affairs committee is less likely to suffer from the "political cast-off syndrome," in which members are placed on a committee just because they need to be appointed to some committee. However, high-profile government affairs committees tend to be more susceptible to personal political agendas (internal and external) of its members.

Types of Committee Members

Government affairs committees are likely to exhibit many of the same group dynamics of other committees. Winston Fletcher, in *Meetings, Meetings* (1984), proposes that committee members can be categorized as follows:

1. **Seers**—people who speak only when they have something worth saying. This is the category to which most of us would like to belong, and most of us believe we do.
2. **Talkies**—people who babble incessantly. A subgroup of this category is the Loudmouths.
3. **Passionates**—people who speak only when they feel the issue is affecting them personally. Passionates run the risk of falling into the subgroup known as the Cracked Records if they do not let go of an issue once the committee has moved on.
4. **Mums**—people who never say anything.
5. **Unknowns**—people who eventually are classified in one of the other four categories, but they have not made their intentions quite clear yet.

Although this is obviously an incomplete list of categories, it does give staff a good foundation from which to gauge committee members. Most of the categories lend themselves to many subgroups.

Identifying Problem Members

Members of government affairs committees also risk suffering from the same flaws as the committee chair, such as a failure to understand the current political climate, extreme personal political and ideological convictions, regionalism, and the inability to see how an issue affects portions of the membership. Although these problems can be worked out with a chair, they pose additional problems in a committee setting because they may pit one member against another.

The best and easiest solution will come about naturally with a chair who knows how to run a good meeting. The chair should allow each committee member to have a say, but the chair should just as forcefully keep the meeting moving toward resolution of the topic at hand. Truly rancorous meetings may require the tried-and-true method of time limits on debates. If this is used, however, the meeting should be consistently run according to proper parliamentary procedure.

One symptom of regionalism in committee members is the consistent use of their own state or locality as a point of reference for every debate. This is probably one of the most common traits of a government affairs committee member because it allows the member to feel comfortable discussing an issue by placing it in a personal context. Although this may only be irritating to other committee members in the beginning, it usually does not stop at this level. The longer an issue is before a committee, the more likely the committee member will become convinced that his or her state or locality has devised the definitive solution to the problem and that it is the proper course for the association to take. Once this happens, it is unlikely that the member will be able to be convinced of any other course of action.

This behavior breeds resentment toward the committee member (and his or her state or hometown) by other members, the chair, and staff and usually leads to this person's views being discounted in future debates. The chair or another committee member should diplomatically approach this member about this behavior and offer suggestions for participating effectively in future debates.

Another example of regionalism is that of members trying to dismiss an issue that they do not perceive as a problem in their state or locality. Again, this situation may call for another member who is affected by the issue to talk to this committee member to place the issue in perspective. A member from the same area as the problem member would be the most persuasive.

Some members of a government affairs committee may have difficulty being team players. This is especially common when the committee adopts a position that is contrary to the position of an individual committee member. This member runs the danger of falling into the "cracked record" subgroup mentioned earlier if he or she refuses to let go of the issue. This member may lobby board members vociferously between meetings to persuade them to reverse the committee's actions. The chair should be prepared to live through the debate again in the board meeting.

Michael P. O'Brien, CAE, and E. Colette Nelson

The committee also may include a "prophet of doom" who has a problem believing the association can succeed on any issue in the public policy arena or believes that adoption of the position in question will be "the first step in opening the floodgates" that will lead to the eventual destruction of the industry. This member eventually will find the "conspiracy theorist" on the committee who believes he or she knows the ultimate motive behind any issue, be it internal or external.

Putting Committee Members to Work

Although it is safe to assume that committee members have an interest in government relations when they are appointed to the committee, the chair may want to exploit that interest even further. One way to do this is to assign issues to individual committee members to monitor and report on at meetings. (The member should have an interest in the issue to which he or she is assigned.) This approach gives committee members a sense of purpose, keeps issues before the whole committee, and reduces the workload of the chair. This system also helps identify future leaders and possible chairs.

Some local associations take a different approach by assigning members the duty of monitoring the actions of a specific local commission, council, agency, and so forth. This helps foster the association's relationship with local government bodies by establishing regular lines of communication.

The Role of Committee Staff

Duties of Staff

There is an old association adage: "If any group of members cannot agree on an issue, it will come to the conclusion that staff is the problem." This would be humorous if it did not ring true. Very little has been written about the role of staff in regard to association committees. Both the U.S. Chamber of Commerce (in *A Guide to Association Committees*) and ASAE (in *Principles of Association Management*) use the same description for the role of committee staff:

> *Staff should render all possible assistance, but should not assume the committee's prerogative. During a committee meeting, the staff representative should be available to answer questions, offer suggestions, or raise questions when appropriate. To this end, staff must be thoroughly familiar with association policy, the committee's scope, and the subject under discussion.*

As most association staff have learned, the staff liaison to association committees is responsible for almost all of the premeeting and postmeeting work and, in the case of the government affairs committee, is the person responsible for lobbying the positions adopted by the committee and board. Usually the staff liaison also is the association's lobbyist.

Many lobbyists do not adapt well to the staff liaison role because it is almost the opposite of the job they were hired to do—lobbying. Lobbyists are comfortable promoting issues and defending positions; therefore, some lobbyists may find it difficult to let the members call the shots in a committee meeting. In addition, many lobbyists do not consider themselves association executives, so they are not necessarily comfortable in the passive duties of preparing for meetings, taking minutes, and speaking when spoken to.

The chief operating officer of the association needs to take this into account when hiring a lobbyist who will be expected to staff a committee. Often, these individuals have just come out of government themselves and are entering a new world. Chief executive officers should be clear with them about their committee responsibilities and should provide them with a checklist of items for meeting preparation.

Performing in Meetings

Government affairs committee staff should conduct "reconnaissance" before meetings. Although it is impossible to anticipate all the actions of committee members, it is possible to find out their positions on controversial issues before meetings. It is staff's responsibility to brief the chair and committee members on the status and impact of issues during the meeting. Committee members should not be voting on any issues on which they have not been fully informed. Such an action could come back to haunt staff at a later date, particularly if the issue takes on increased political significance.

During meetings, staff should give concise reports and answers to any questions posed. Staff should avoid lobbying jargon so as not to confuse members who probably will be too embarrassed to question what it means. But they should not pull any punches about the reality of the political landscape. That is the kind of knowledge the association is paying them for, and it should be discussed before the committee adopts policy recommendations.

Staff should avoid appearing to promote their personal views on issues. They should present the facts, including the chances for success or failure, and let the committee members make the decision. Staff should make clear what association resources are available to support the action of the committee. If something cannot be accomplished because of insufficient money, staff, or time, then the committee members should be made aware of those factors.

Preparing the Minutes

Staff usually are responsible for the minutes of the meetings. Although many people claim that minutes are never read, they usually are read when the actual events of the meeting can no longer be remembered. Minutes also have been known to save a staff person's job when his or her actions have been questioned.

Minutes should be prepared promptly after the meeting and should state who was present, what decisions were made, follow-up required, motions passed or defeated, and summary of discussion. Minutes should be distributed to all committee members after the meeting.

Michael P. O'Brien,
CAE, and
E. Colette Nelson

Achieving Consensus in Government Affairs Committees

Defining Consensus

The word "consensus" often is used to describe the association decision-making process. Unfortunately, the word rarely means the same thing to any two associations because the word is not easy to define. Even *Webster's Dictionary* provides only a vague definition: "group solidarity in sentiment and belief."

There is no standard formula for achieving consensus in government affairs committees because the composition of the committee, the composition of the association, and the size of the membership all will directly affect the consensus process. A small association of members performing the same work in the same geographic area probably will have an easier time achieving consensus than a large association with a diverse membership dispersed across the country. The small association will have a narrower focus and less issues of direct concern.

Using a Consensus Process

Government affairs committees should have no more than fifteen to twenty members. The more members involved in the committee, the more difficult it will be to achieve consensus on issues. Some associations may have by-laws that mandate the number of committee members allowed.

Committee members should be representative of the association membership as a whole in terms of the types of work performed and geographic areas. Task forces, subcommittees, and working groups of the full committee should be formed sparingly and with a lot of thought as to their mission, focus, and life span. All subcommittees should have a definite life span; otherwise the association could wind up creating a bureaucracy that rivals the government and bogs down the association.

The consensus development process in government affairs committees requires a lot of premeeting preparation. The goal of every staff person is to be able to predict the outcome of policy votes. That is done by using the premeeting reconnaissance mentioned earlier.

Before considering any issue, staff should collect as many facts as possible on the issue's status, impact, and chances for passage or adoption. Staff also should be aware of any current association policies that may already cover the issue in question or that may conflict with the proposed policy. The chair should be briefed ahead of time about all these factors. On potentially divisive issues, staff and/or the chair should take a brief survey of committee members' premeeting attitudes toward the issue. If time allows, a written membership survey about the issue often provides useful information during policy development.

During the committee meeting, all members should be given the opportunity to voice their opinion, and the policy should be revised as necessary. Debate should not be stifled merely because the chair or some committee members are bored or have somewhere else to go (which is an extra burden when the meeting is taking place in a resort area). Debate that is stopped prematurely will breed resentment among those who were cut off and could lead to more problems at the next level of consideration. Every effort should be made to ensure the decision-making process is open and that there is no appearance of impropriety.

Michael P. O'Brien,
CAE, and
E. Colette Nelson

28

Dissenters

In *Lobbying and Government Relations* (1989), Charles Mack points out another problem of the committee decision-making process: "A committee decision has a few characteristic disadvantages of its own. If it is unanimous, there arises a concern that both sides of the question were not fairly represented. If the decision is a fair compromise, and it is probably not even a majority opinion, it may well be a decision that pleases nobody."

This raises the question of what to do about hard core dissenters. In the association consensus process, there always is the danger that a member will publicly repudiate the position of the association. This may be an extreme and rare occurrence for most associations, but it is common in large associations that have a diverse national membership. In these instances, it would be wise for the association to develop a formal process that requires a member who is going to publicly repudiate a position of the association to first notify the association's leadership.

Most dissenters are likely to work internally to change the position at the next level of consideration, which is their democratic right. However, if they do so by making charges of collusion and conspiracy, the chair would be wise to speak to the person about his or her actions. Most members want peer approval too much to use underhanded tactics, but they may feel comfortable attacking staff with charges of collusion.

Prioritizing Issues

The sheer number of issues in the government arena requires a system for prioritizing the issues in terms of time, staff, and resources. There is no perfect system of prioritizing issues. Any system that meets the needs of the association is a good system. The important thing is to have some system of prioritizing. Some prioritizing systems are relatively simple, while others can get quite complex. Many associations rank issues with a number or letter (see Table 3-1).

Table 3-1. **Sample Prioritizing System**

+3 =	Support issue by testifying, sending letters, using grassroots, lobbying
+2 =	Support issue by testifying, sending letters
+1 =	Support issue by sending letters, joining coalitions
0 =	No position adopted
−1 =	Oppose issue by sending letters, joining coalitions
−2 =	Oppose issue by testifying, sending letters
−3 =	Oppose issue by testifying, sending letters, using grassroots, lobbying

Although a numbering or lettering system can be useful in the committee voting process, it is really the criteria for arriving at those rankings that are complicated. A systematic process with defined criteria should be used to develop those rankings. For government affairs committee members, a system gives them concrete guidelines when making assessments about a broad range of issues. By using a well-thought-out and formalized system, committee members can justify their decisions based on the impact the issue will have on the association's membership.

Conclusion

The committee process is the heart and soul of most associations. On the surface, the committee structure may look like a simple way to make decisions, but most staff have discovered otherwise. Government affairs committees are no less complicated than other association committees, and they have some unique aspects that set them apart from other committees. If they are managed with care and preparation, they can help the association achieve its government relations goals and better serve the membership.

BIBLIOGRAPHY

American Society of Association Executives. 1990. *Getting involved: The challenge of committee participation.* Washington, D.C.: American Society of Association Executives.

American Society of Association Executives. 1990. *Principles of Association Management,* Second Edition. Washington, D.C.: American Society of Association Executives.

Fletcher, Winston. 1984. *Meetings, meetings: How to manipulate them and make them more fun.* New York: William Morrow & Co.

Mack, Charles. 1989. *Lobbying and government relations.* Westport, CT: Quorum Books.

Perlov, Dadie. 1990. "Achieving legislative consensus in individual membership organizations." In *Beyond Washington: An association guide to shaping a state government affairs program.* Washington, D.C.: American Society of Association Executives.

Ross, Sarah Meyerdierks. June 1982. "Forming legislative policy: Democracy at work." *Association Management.*

U.S. Chamber of Commerce. 1987. *A guide to association committees.* Washington, D.C.: U.S. Chamber of Commerce.

Westendorf, William H. 1990. "Achieving legislative consensus in trade associations," in *Beyond Washington: An association guide to shaping a state government affairs program.* Washington, D.C.: American Society of Association Executives.

Michael P. O'Brien, CAE, and E. Colette Nelson

CHAPTER 4

Funding Your Government Relations Program

Brian Pallasch, CAE

AN ASSOCIATION GOVERNMENT RELATIONS DEPARTMENT, whether large or small, is not a revenue-generating center. Unlike the membership department or publications department, the government relations department has few ways to generate revenue—there are few products to sell or sponsorship dollars to attract.

In fact, government relations costs money—sometimes a lot of money. Therefore, to be successful, many government relations professionals are faced with seeking additional money to fund the government relations program.

Creating the Fund-raising Environment

Raising money for a government relations program is not as easy as just asking. Before beginning a fund-raising campaign, groundwork must be done to ensure the success of the campaign. Essentially, an environment for fund-raising must be created, and there are several key steps involved.

The first step to creating a positive fund-raising environment is communication. Association members must know the mission of the government relations department and how it affects their bottom line.

The association's publications should be used extensively to communicate the activities of the government relations program. When possible, create and produce special publications to communicate the government relations message. It is important that members know what the government relations department is doing, how it affects their businesses, and how they are a part of that success.

The second step in successful fund-raising is getting the buy-in of the members and, more important, the association leadership. Creating buy-in takes time and effort. To build support, educate board members and chapter leaders (if a chapter structure exists) about how the government relations program operates. Tell members exactly what you do and how you do it.

Show these key members the efforts of the government relations department's focus on ensuring that the government does not make business or life activities more difficult for association members. The American Subcontractors Association (ASA), Alexandria, Va., has fostered chapter buy-in of its government relations program by creating a training program for newly hired chapter executive directors. During the orientation program, the new executive directors meet with every congressional office in their chapter's area. Not only does this provide them with contacts in Washington, D.C., but it also gives ASA's government relations staff a chance to educate the new executive directors about the government relations program firsthand.

The third step in creating a positive fund-raising environment is demonstrating how the government relations program supports the association's overall goals. The activities of the government relations program must support the association's mission. It is the job of a government relations professional to link the government relations activities back to the organization's goals and objectives. This becomes easier when an association has a well-defined strategic plan with a clear set of goals and objectives.

Alternative Sources of Funding

Once a positive environment for fund-raising has been created, the various sources of funds available to an association government relations program can be examined. These include:

- increasing dues;
- charging a special assessment for each major issue;
- dedicating nondues revenue to government relations; and
- creating a government relations fund.

Increasing dues

The most direct route to raising money for the government relations program is to increase membership dues and dedicate the additional funds to the government relations program. Because dues increases are a difficult, if not impossible, sell, this is a controversial option. It also may be the most difficult way to raise money. In many associations, raising the cost of dues is a cumbersome and highly political process that creates acrimony among members. In addition, future boards of directors may decide to move the funds out of the government relations department. This option, like any fundraising option, must be thoroughly debated among the association leadership before it is chosen. The amount to raise dues is determined after the association has established how much additional revenue is necessary to fund the government relations program.

Charging a special assessment for each major issue

Another dues-oriented way to tackle the problem is to place a special assessment on members when a key issue arises. This generally is only a short-term solution to the funding problem, but it can assist the association in playing an active role in a key legislative or regulatory battle. It is not, however, without risks—members can vote with their wallets and not support a special assessment if there is controversy over the association's position on the issue. In many associations, the special assessment is not mandatory, but this can be determined by the Board of Directors or may be set forth in the association's bylaws.

Dedicating nondues revenue to government relations

Today most associations have several nondues revenue streams ranging from royalty agreements with credit card companies and shipping companies to insurance programs. The association may decide to dedicate some or all of these revenues to the government relations program.

Nondues income can be used for a government relations program in any of several ways. One would be to dedicate all or a portion of an association's nondues revenue to the government relations program regardless of the sources of the revenue. A second way would be to dedicate all nondues revenue generated by the government relations department to funding the government relations department. A government relations department can generate nondues revenue by charging registration fees for its legislative conference, creating compliance tools for newly issued government regulations, or instituting sponsorships for the legislative conference and other government relations education programs. These examples of using nondues revenue can be mixed and matched to create the proper fit for most associations.

Creating a government relations fund

Another source of funding is one that a government relations department can create and manage itself—a government relations fund. The American Society of Association Executives (ASAE) has a fund of this type called the Association Alliance.

The Association Alliance was created to help ASAE pay for its public advocacy program and supplement funds from ASAE's general fund. In fiscal year 1996 alone, ASAE raised more than $400,000 to fund its government relations program from Association Alliance contributions.

Brian Pallasch, CAE

In many instances, special government relations funds are separate, but not necessarily segregated, from the association's general fund. The government relations department usually is responsible for raising the money and managing the fund.

The advantages of a separate fund are that members know exactly what they are contributing to and the benefits are easily communicated. If the separate fund produced a key lobbying campaign or funded a special lobbying fly-in that made a significant difference for members, this can be easily touted.

Depending on the issues faced by the association, it also may be worthwhile to create a legal defense fund. More and more associations are being forced to use the third branch of government to further the goals of the government relations program. (See chapter 15, "Adding the Courts to Your Lobbying Arsenal.") Creating a legal defense fund is an ideal way to use the concept of a special fund to augment the activities of the government relations program.

A government relations program can use just one of these types of fund-raisers, or a combination. The choice can be made when it is determined how much money is needed to fund the program

Other Types of Fund-raising

It may be possible to use some other tried-and-true fund-raising techniques usually reserved for foundations and political action committees to fund a government relations programs. Examples of these include in-kind services, special events (for example, golf tournaments or dinner programs at conventions), auctions (silent or live), novelties, and sponsorships.

How Much Money Do You Need?

After exploring the types of funding available, it is important examine the government relations program to determine how much money is necessary to make the program successful and meet members' needs. To determine a budget, it is necessary to identify the association's issues and set priorities according to the members' needs. (See chapter 2, "Issue Development: A Strategic Marketing Approach.") This can be done by the government relations committee in coordination with the board of directors and may include direct member involvement through surveys or focus groups.

Once priorities are set, a budget can be drafted. Items that should be included are staff, travel, communications (fax broadcasting, Internet, newsletters), meetings, subscriptions, and so forth.

Additionally, it is necessary to determine what resources are available from the association's general fund. Once the board of directors has determined what is available from the general fund, it is easy to determine how much outside revenue must be raised to fully fund the government relations program.

Prioritization plays a key role. If priorities are set realistically, the budgeting process can be used to fund high priorities from general funds and leave lesser priorities to those funds that are less certain.

Establishing a Special Government Relations Fund

As association funds become hard fought, many government relations departments are creating special funds to supplement the funds received from the association's general fund. The following is a blueprint that can be used to create a special government relations fund.

First, as with the government relations program in general, it is necessary to get buy-in from the association's leadership. After buy-in is achieved, it is necessary to create a set of policies that identifies what is funded by the government relations fund and who controls it. These policies allow the association to focus the fund and keep it in line with government relations priorities. The following is a sample policy statement:

1. The Government Relations Fund (GRF) is a separate, segregated account under the management and control of the association board of directors and the existing corporate structure.

2. The GRF is under the direction of the Government Relations Committee. A GRF subcommittee of the full committee should be created. The association president is an *ex officio,* nonvoting member of the subcommittee.

3. To use the GRF, the government relations committee, board of directors, and chapters must submit to the association president and chair of the Government Relations Committee the following:
    (a) detailed proposal of how the funds will be used;
    (b) expected outcomes;
    (c) project budget; and
    (d) time frame in which program will be completed.

4. The subcommittee will confer within a reasonable time after receipt of the request. The committee will evaluate requests according to the following criteria:
    (a) The issues are of specific interest to association members.
    (b) The issues are focused and clearly presented.
    (c) There is a consensus among members on the issues.
    (d) The association could have a meaningful impact on the outcome.
    (e) The issues or forums are of high visibility from a public relations standpoint.

5. The subcommittee will:
    (a) decide whether or not to provide funds;
    (b) set maximum funds to be committed or provided by the fund for the project;
    (c) establish the basis for and approve all disbursements from the fund; and
    (d) notify the association's Executive Committee of its decisions.

6. Any decision by the Government Relations subcommittee is subject to veto by the Executive Committee, provided such veto occurs within ten days (or shorter time if required by the judicial schedule) after the Executive Committee receives notice of the subcommittee's decision.

With a policy in place, it is now possible to begin raising funds for the government relations fund. The following fund-raising guidelines can be adapted to any association's needs.

Identification—The fund-raising effort should be easily recognizable and remembered. If this is going to be a long-term campaign, a special logo and brochure should be created.

Packaging—Members should understand the issue and its importance to the association. All fund-raising materials should include a clear explanation of the fund; it is especially important to explain how the funds will be used.

Identify a fund-raising team—Key association members should be asked to help raise funds. Teams can be created by dividing the membership by geographic region, industry, or membership type. Once this has been done, fund-raising volunteers should be assigned to each segmented group. When raising funds this way, it is important to use the member's letterhead if at all possible. This personalizes the appeal, and the fund-raising pitch does not get lost in the large volume of association mail received by most association members.

Pricing—Set an appropriate contribution scale. The worst mistake in fund-raising is to ask for too little money. One method used successfully by several groups, including ASAE and ASA, is a sliding scale based on a member's revenue. This helps ensure that money is not left on the table. (See Table 4-1 for a sample sliding scale.)

Table 4-1. **Sample Sliding Scale**

Company's Annual Sales	Suggested Contribution
$100,000 – $499,999	$100
$500,000 – $999,999	$250
$1,000,000 – $2,999,999	$500
$3,000,000 – $6,999,999	$750
$7,000,000 – $9,999,999	$1,000
$10,000,000 plus	$2,500

Communication—Give members periodic updates on the progress of the association's fund-raising efforts. Send a thank-you letter to each contributor as soon as the contribution is received. More important, recognize contributors and let them know how the funds raised are being spent. This information should be included in all appropriate association publications. An annual report for the fund should include a list of contributors and details of how the fund was used in the previous year.

Conclusion

Regardless of the type of alternative funding mechanism chosen, it is important that it not be the only source of funding for your government relations program. The core costs of a government relations program should be covered with funds from the association's general account. This alone makes government relations an integral part of the association's mission and creates a certain level of buy-in.

Fund-raising takes a tremendous amount of time, and government relations professionals with multiple responsibilities should be careful not to fall into the trap of spending so much time raising money that they cannot protect the interests of the association's members.

Brian Pallasch, CAE

CHAPTER 5

Creating and Operating a Government Relations Program on a Small Budget

Michael E. Kastner

GOVERNMENT RELATIONS PROGRAMS generally are created in response to an actual or perceived need for representation before one or more governments. Your concerns may be local, state, federal, or international in origin. You may have legislative or regulatory interests. You could have a wide-ranging combination of government relations needs encompassing all of those areas. It may be that you are seeing more and more government regulations adversely affecting your industry or members. Whatever your specific area of government relations concern, the decision to create a government relations program for your association is primarily an economic one.

Often, associations initiate their government relations activities by retaining a law firm or lobbyist to address one specific issue that directly affects their membership. This type of relationship may work well for many associations on a permanent basis. However, the association's members often begin to recognize the benefits of government relations involvement and become interested in expanding the program.

When deciding whether to stretch your government relations activities beyond a single issue or specific piece of legislation, the association needs to decide how best to accomplish this goal. It may be that an expanded contract relationship will work. On the other hand, if you want to significantly broaden the scope of your activities, an in-house government relations program should be considered.

An in-house government relations department, even if it consists of just one person, generally can accomplish more at a lower cost than could a contract lobbyist or law firm. A dedicated full- or part-time government relations professional can do things that wouldn't make sense if done by a consultant at an hourly rate. An in-house lobbyist is likely to become involved in industry coalitions and peripheral events, such as receptions or fund-raising. Your own government relations department also is more likely to be able to more readily and thoroughly monitor trends and work proactively than a contract lobbyist or law firm at a similar cost.

Government Relations on a Small Budget

Every association government relations program, big or small, must set priorities. Regardless of the level of funding, no organization will be able to do everything. However, prioritization is especially critical for government relations on a shoestring budget. Government relations practitioners with limited staff and financial resources have to be even better at prioritizing than those who have more significant funds with which to work.

You will need to make several difficult decisions to ensure the best return on your association's investment. You will need to make some equally hard choices in determining and achieving your association's government relations goals. You need to accept the fact that you can't do everything and determine which achievable goals will help your members the most.

Get your board of directors or government relations committee together and decide what you should try to accomplish. Your initial goal should be to provide tangible results for your members—results that will improve your members' bottom line or their primary reason for being. These types of successes early on will help ensure the continued existence and prosperity of your government relations program.

Don't spread yourself too thin, you'll end up accomplishing little or nothing, other than spending the association's money. Choose issues you will be able to affect positively within the confines of your program and will make a difference to your members.

Your members should be involved from the very start. Use them as resources to develop your positions and strategies. The more involved your members are in developing the association's position, the more likely they are to carry your message with true conviction.

When your government relations investment starts paying dividends through demonstrable victories, make sure everyone—especially members—knows about them. If your members are unaware of your government relations victories, they might as well not have occurred. The more excited and proud your members are about the government relations function, the more involved they will become in it. And the more involved your members are in the government relations program, the more successful it will become.

How Much Money Do We Need?

A government relations program does not have to be an enormous drain on an association's budget. Although government relations may not be able to pay for itself within the confines of the association's revenue stream, a good government relations program can provide a significant return on investment to the association's members.

When setting up a budget, be realistic. Don't set your sights too high or, even worse, too low. If you currently have a contract lobbyist or law firm doing your government relations work, start with that budget. How best could you reallocate those funds for an in-house program?

As part of your budget process, you need to consider what your government relations department wants to accomplish in both the short term and the long term. You want to be sure that your budget will allow a realistic chance of accomplishing your goals or, conversely, that your goals are realistic in consideration of your budget.

The surest way for your in-house government relations department experiment to fail is to not provide enough money for accomplishing the goals you have publicly set. The other sure way to fail is to sell your membership and board on a set of unrealistic government relations goals.

Your budget should take into account many of the same things any budget covers: staff, office space, and travel. You also should consider the possible cost of member and, perhaps, general public grassroots efforts, coalition building, public relations, gathering of industry or membership statistics, and research to bolster your positions.

Office Location

If your association is headquartered in the capital city, you probably will want to simply locate your government relations department in your existing facility. If your association is not located in convenient proximity to the people you need to lobby, there are several options.

First, you could still locate your government relations department in your existing facility. In this case, you will need to consider the cost of travel and lodging. Also be aware that it is more difficult for your lobbyists to be effective when they are geographically separated from the people they need to lobby. Things often happen quickly, and if you aren't nearby, you will need to adapt. It also will be more difficult for your government relations professionals to become involved with coalition-type activities when they are located outside the capital area.

Office options for a satellite government relations department include executive office suites, office sublets, shared office space, and home offices.

Executive office suites. Executive office suites offer one-stop office shopping. Depending on the facility, they may offer individual offices, meeting space, secretarial services, a phone receptionist, and office equipment. Such offices and services generally can be rented on a permanent or temporary basis. One firm even rents offices by the hour. This type of arrangement may be particularly suited to government relations professionals operating out of their home or an association that is not headquartered nearby and who need only temporary or occasional office and meeting space in the capital area.

Office sublets and shared offices. If permanent office space is needed in the capital area, consider office sublets or sharing. An affiliated association that is headquartered in the capital area may have office space available for rent. You may be able to work out a deal for office services as well. Similarly, you may do business with a law firm or a supplier who is appropriately located and able to sublet office space. There may be other associations in your field who are considering setting up government relations departments. If so, consider sharing office space and services.

Home offices. Home offices can work well. If you have a one-person government relations department, you may not need formal office space. Some people consider working out of their home to be a great benefit. Be cautious, however, because not everyone feels this way and not everyone works well from his or her home. If you do choose to use the home-office concept, be aware that formal meeting space may be required at times.

When money is tight, being creative is typically rewarded. Don't assume that a government relations program requires sumptuous offices overlooking Capitol Hill.

How Many Staff People Do We Need?

If you are just starting your government relations department, chances are it is going to be with one full-time professional, or less. Ideally, your government relations professional should be dedicated to that function alone.

However, you may need to start your department with a person who also wears other association hats. In this case, be sure to quantify what portion of that person's time should be dedicated to government relations functions, and keep to that schedule. When your budget cannot accommodate a full-time professional for your government relations department, you may want to consider a dedicated part-time employee. There are many well-qualified professionals who choose to work part-time rather than full-time.

Assuming your budget allows for them, administrative staff can be used quite effectively in a government relations program. If you are on a small budget and have support staff, choose them wisely. Support staff need to do more than take messages and stuff envelopes. Hire people with an interest in politics or knowledge of your membership. Get them involved in what you do, send them to hearings, and let them compose grassroots communications. Always train your support staff to do jobs at a level higher than their actual job.

Encourage other association employees to become interested in and involved with the government relations function. Educate the staff of other departments about your job, how you do it, and the benefits it provides to the association's members. Demystify the political and lobbying process and strive to provide all association staff with a feeling of ownership in your association's government relations victories.

Consider using volunteers and student interns to supplement the association's employees' efforts. Volunteers from the association membership understand your member's needs and concerns. Members can form a grassroots army and be the eyes and ears in the field. Members also may be willing to do research for you or to draft position papers. When you need an expert for legislative testimony or lobbying, your members are the obvious choice. Select a few members, and cultivate their talents.

College student interns also can be valuable. They can bring energy and a fresh perspective. Provide them with a mix of administrative and professional tasks. Set realistic expectations for their participation. Keep in mind that they will be with you for only a limited amount of time, so long-term training is not advisable unless you expect them back. Give both your interns and your administrative staff exposure to association members. It helps to make them feel a part of the team and increases the likelihood your association leadership will consider promoting or hiring them as full-time professionals. If you demonstrate that your administrative staff and interns contribute significantly to your government relations program's success, you may increase the odds of being able to hire additional government relations staff.

Do We Need a Political Action Committee?

It is not necessary to have a political action committee (PAC), but there are some advantages to having one even if it isn't well funded. (For more information about PACs, see chapter 11, "Political Action Committees and Campaign Involvement.") Although a PAC creates a certain paperwork and reporting burden, once it is up and running, it won't be much of an administrative burden if all your contributions in and out are fairly straightforward. However, you should seek professional advice when setting up your PAC.

A PAC should be viewed as one more government relations tool in your arsenal. In the long run, a strong PAC will help you be successful. It will get members involved and interested in government relations, and it will open up additional avenues in which to interact with legislators and their staff.

Even a small PAC that makes few contributions can be valuable. Once you have a PAC, numerous invitations will come your way. Most of these invitations will be to fund-raisers you may choose not to attend; however, some invitations will be for less formal meet-and-greet events. These events don't cost anything and give you an opportunity to speak with political candidates. You also will find that candidates and their parties will funnel a lot of election research your way. This information can be valuable to you as a lobbyist and would not have been delivered to your doorstep if it weren't for your PAC.

You also may want to consider charitable contributions as a part of your government relations program. Many legislators are actively involved with charities. By supporting these charities, your association and its members will not only help the charitable organization but also open up yet another avenue in which to interact with the legislator. A strong and consistent charitable support program can also raise the visibility of your association within the community as a whole.

With or without a PAC, encourage individual association members to become involved with election efforts in their home districts. An association member's personal relationship with a key legislator is worth more than dozens of lobbyists. What better way to develop that personal relationship than helping the legislator get elected?

Coalitions

Join coalitions. Coalitions are a great way to pool resources and information. Many coalitions will be fully funded by larger organizations that have a greater vested interest in the issue than does your association. These coalitions can provide you with research and political intelligence that would be too expensive or time consuming to gather on your own. In return, your association typically lends its name as a supporter of the coalition's goals and provides the coalition with greater grassroots strength. The amount of lobbying you actually conduct on behalf of the coalition should be based on your organization's priorities.

Typically, the more directly an issue affects your members, the more direct lobbying you will want to conduct. The strength of the coalition can affect how you allocate your resources. If the coalition is strong and broad based, you may want to consider letting them carry more of your water. On the other hand, if the coalition is small or only partially covers your concerns, you may need to increase the level of your direct lobbying activities.

Technology

Embrace technology. Computers can help you in almost every aspect of lobbying. You can prepare and communicate grassroots information quickly with computers. You can do more research through the Internet than you could do in any library, and you never have to leave your desk. You can then write up and distribute that research from the same computer.

The daily *Congressional Record* and *Federal Register* are available online at no cost, other than whatever your Internet provider charges for access. Cancel your paper subscriptions, and save several hundred

Creating and
Operating a
Government
Relations
Program on a
Small Budget

45

dollars a year and countless shelf space. Legislative status and committee reports are available with just a few clicks of the computer's mouse. Federal regulatory agencies also have Web sites that provide copies of press releases, testimony, and research papers that can be viewed or downloaded. Many individual states offer similar access.

This technological revolution is a double-edged sword. You can be more knowledgeable and productive as a result of all this information. You also can be overloaded by it. Be selective. Find out what is available, and decide what is really going to help you do a better job.

Remember that whatever information is available to you via the Internet also is available to your members. You may have already received a call from a member asking what you have done about a bill that was introduced yesterday and of which you are completely unaware. You may find yourself explaining over and over again to your members that just because a bill is introduced does not necessarily mean it will become law. Nonetheless, encourage these members. They have demonstrated an interest in government relations and should make good grassroots soldiers.

Grassroots

Computer technology lends itself to grassroots mobilization. You can identify association members in a congressional district through zip code matching software. You can pull up committee or subcommittee lists easily. You can distribute your legislative alerts through electronic mail (e-mail) in minutes.

E-mail can be an important tool for grassroots organizers. However, caution is advised. You may want to use broadcast fax technology to send legislative newsletters and alerts instead of mailing them. However, you will find that some members still want or need to receive your newsletter by mail. If you move from broadcast fax to e-mail, the same thing is likely to occur. Some members will still want or need the newsletter by broadcast fax (or by mail). You may find that, instead of just mailing everything, you now have three distribution lists: one each for mail, broadcast fax, and e-mail. However, it's still worth making the change. Typically, broadcast fax is faster and cheaper than mail, and e-mail is faster and cheaper than broadcast fax. Push your members' technology. It will benefit everyone.

If you send out legislative alerts via e-mail, your members may assume that sending a letter to their legislator via e-mail also is appropriate. Generally speaking, that is not the way to go. A personal phone call or letter via the mail or fax is still better. Everyone's e-mail looks the same. In addition, many legislators have yet to warm up to e-mail and don't necessarily look at it on a regular basis. Also, your technologically advanced members should be cautioned about contacting every legislator via e-mail just because it is easy enough to do. Legislators may not like having their e-mail system flooded by letters from people outside their district.

Consultants as Money Savers

In many instances, consultants, law firms, and contract lobbyists can save you money. This could seem as if you are coming full circle— you may have started your in-house government relations department because it was becoming too expensive to outsource the government relations function. Judiciously used, however, independent consultants can save time and money. (See chapter 6, "Hiring and Managing Contract Lobbyists," for more information.)

It may make sense to hire a contract lobbyist if an unfamiliar issue comes up before a legislative committee with which you have few contacts. It may not be possible to develop the necessary contacts on a timely basis or learn the ins and outs of a specific issue. In these cases, it often makes sense to contract with someone who has the right skills and can hit the ground running.

It may be prudent to outsource research you hope to use as ammunition for your legislative strategy. Research studies from an independent group tend to appear more credible. Additionally, your organization simply may not be qualified to conduct the research.

Consider outsourcing routine tasks. Depending on your association's capabilities, it may make sense to outsource your legislative newsletter or other grassroots communications. You want your government relations professionals to spend their time lobbying and developing strategy, not stuffing legislative alerts in envelopes.

Conclusion

An association's government relations program does not need to be expensive. Using technology and finding creative ways to deliver your message can keep costs down. Getting your membership involved is the key. Your members need to see the value in government relations. When they consider government relations to be a valuable association service, they will do more of your work for you: they will write letters and make phone calls. They will come to the capital and testify for you. Most important, they will keep government relations at the top of the association's priority list.

NOTE

Milton Bush, JD, CAE, of The 'M Companies and Wayne Curtin of Liberty Associates also contributed information for the preparation of this chapter.

Hiring and Managing Contract Lobbyists

Marcie M. McNelis, CAE

LOBBYING IS FUNDAMENTAL to the legislative process. It's how information is delivered and how arguments are made. Furthermore, it is how decisions are reached by the "Body Politick." Everyone lobbies. Legislators lobby for their own bills; the governor or president lobbies for his or her agenda, departments, and agencies; consumers and manufacturers, foreign interests, patient groups and medical providers, students, professors, book publishers...everyone lobbies. The issue is not whether to lobby, but rather how to do it effectively and ethically. How do you create a coordinated lobbying effort without devoting huge resources to putting professional government relations staff in Washington, D.C., and in state capitals across the country? If you cannot be there yourself, and often even if you can be, the services of a professional contract lobbyist can make the difference between winning and losing your issue.

What Are Contract Lobbyists?

Contract lobbyists are independent professional advocates who typically represent multiple clients before legislative and/or executive branches of government on an outsourced basis. They come in many different forms. Many are sole practitioners; others work in law/lobbying firms or in group practices where they represent some clients individually and team with colleagues on others. Many are lawyers, former legislators, or former legislative staff or executive branch officials.

If the lobbyist is an attorney in a firm, the firm may be a law practice as well, particularly in the states, where legislative sessions extend anywhere from thirty days to all year, with intermittent recesses. Law firms with significant lobbying practices often create public affairs subsidiaries to accommodate nonlawyer lobbyists who are associated with the government relations side of the practice.

Basic Functions of a Contract Lobbyist

Lobbying today is considerably more technical, broad based, and time consuming than it was just a few decades ago. Gone are the days when being close to the House speaker or the Senate president meant lobbyists could accomplish their legislative goals with a few phone calls. Today, legislatures are dealing with increasingly complicated issues in a fishbowl of participatory democracy activated by grassroots campaigns and the playing out of issues in the media. High turnover in legislatures, from Congress to the smallest state capitals, means loss of institutional memory and requires continuous education of elected (and appointed) officials on your issues.

Clients retain contract lobbyists to provide access, relationships, experience, strategies, professional advice, and the ability to use these talents and implement these strategies. Typically, you will want your lobbyist to:

- identify issues that impact your association's members;

- deliver on-site intelligence about the political circumstances surrounding an issue;

- provide knowledge of the legislative process and the unique culture of that particular legislative or regulatory body;

- bring credibility that a local, trusted participant in the process has earned through years of interaction with legislators and regulators;

- facilitate access to legislators;

- develop a strategy for your legislative campaign, and where necessary and available, provide direction on when to "pull the trigger" and where to target grassroots and public relations efforts to support the campaign; and

- advocate the client's position day in and day out as legislation moves through the legislative process and to the president's or governor's desk.

Preplanning—
Do You Need a Contract Lobbyist?

Before retaining a professional lobbyist, the threshold question is, "Do I need outside counsel?" In most cases, there is no point in mounting an effort if you know you cannot win. Therefore, you must ask yourself, "Is it doable?" You must do some soul-searching if your issue is proactive; that is, if you're trying to get a bill passed or a policy adopted. It is usually far easier to defeat a bill than to get one passed, because there are numerous places a bill can be stopped, while it has to clear every hurdle to pass. In fact, only 5 percent of the 6,542 bills introduced in the 104th Congress actually passed. At the state level, approximately 25 percent of the 187,000 bills in a typical biennium pass.

The answer to whether you need a lobbyist may depend on the type of issue and the state. For example, if licensing for your association's profession is your cause, you will find Vermont a difficult state in which to achieve your objective, whereas in South Carolina, licensing any and all professions is typical.

You must first carefully study the history of your issue. Has it been considered and defeated many times in recent history? Have there been any significant changes in political dynamics since the issue was last aired, such as the departure of a recalcitrant leader opposed to your position? Was the issue just up last session and resolved, but not to your liking?

Consider your timing. Is this the best year to pursue the issue? Remember that the even-numbered, nonpresidential year is the big election year for state legislators and governors. If your issue requires political courage, you may find political courage in short supply in an election year.

Consider whether it is the first or second year of the legislative session, particularly if your campaign is a proactive one. (Congress and forty-one of the forty-three states with biennial sessions begin the biennium in the odd-numbered year; New Jersey and Virginia begin their biennial session in the even-numbered year.) In some states, fiscal matters command either the first or the second year of the session, and waiting for the nonbudget year may be helpful, if you have the luxury of time. Circumstances often will dictate when you can be proactive. Louisiana, for example, reserves the second year of the regular session for fiscal matters only.

In many states, the second year of the biennium is a shorter session, and politicking for the fall election may dominate the legislative agenda, particularly in legislative chambers where a swing of a few seats would switch party control. Seven states are in session only every other year: Arkansas, Montana, Nevada, North Dakota, Oregon, and Texas have no regular session in even-numbered years; Kentucky has no regular session in odd-numbered years. Thus, unless your issue is germane to the subject of a special session called by the governor, you will have to wait until the next regular session in these states.

Look at your organization as well. Are you known in the state? If not, you may want to spend time educating legislators about your business and building visibility; it may be more effective to wait until a subsequent year to hire a lobbyist.

Also ask yourself whether you have what it takes to do the job internally. You should consider financial resources, staff, and time. Do you have the political connections to do it yourself? How deep are those connections? For example, if you will rely on your relationship with the speaker or the governor, can you afford for it to get that far? Take an inventory of the resources available to accomplish your objective. Consider grassroots, coalitions, and political action committee funds.

It is difficult to understand the unique culture and rules of fifty different state legislatures and be successful in representing your association's views as an outsider. If you do not have professional staff and a well-organized and well-directed grassroots army on the ground in a state—and many times even if you do have these resources—the services of a professional contract lobbyist can be the most effective and efficient tool in your government relations toolbox. The bottom line is that you need a quarterback—someone to make it happen.

Where Do You Find a Contract Lobbyist?

Once you have established that you need a contract lobbyist and you have defined clear objectives for what you want to achieve by using an outside lobbyist, the next challenge is to find the right person.

Some resources available to help identify a potential contract lobbyist include the following:

- Federal and state lobbyist registration lists are available at the federal level from the clerk of the House and from various directories of Washington representatives. State lists are available from either the Secretary of State's office or the Ethics Commission, depending on where lobbyists must register. You can use these lists to find names and addresses of lobbyists and to learn who their clients are.

Marcie M. McNelis, CAE

- Your own association members and staff, and those of allied associations, may be helpful.

- The Chamber of Commerce tends to recommend business lobbyists. This is not a problem; just make sure they are on your side.

- Recommendations from others who have lobbied or currently lobby full-time on behalf of a single employer are helpful.

- Legislative leaders may be a good source, but consider the consequences if they make a recommendation and you decide on another selection. Rank-and-file legislators are perhaps a safer source, but some do not like being put in a position of recommending a lobbyist on a bill on which they will be voting because their suggestion may be misconstrued as improper or a conflict of interest. Also consider legislative staff.

- Government affairs consulting firms, which maintain a network of contract lobbyists in all state capitals, can save you time and money and be valuable consultants as well. Should you decide to go to an outside firm, make sure that there is no charge for the proposal—that it costs no more to work through them than it would cost you to do it yourself, that they are a resource and part of your team (not just a headhunter), that they have in-depth state experience themselves, and that their network is deep and broad enough to bring you the right person for your particular issue.

Remember, you are hiring access, relationships, experience, ideas, strategies, professional advice, and the ability to make things happen.

What to Consider When Hiring a Contract Lobbyist

Characteristics of a Good Lobbyist

Many of the basic characteristics you seek in a contract lobbyist are the same as those you want in an employee. In addition, you are hiring them for their specific experience, expertise, and contacts in the particular legislative arena in which you need representation. Critical assets include:

- integrity and credibility;
- complete knowledge of and record of compliance with the lobbying ethics laws;
- access to key players;.

- knowledge of the legislative process;
- strong communications skills;
- the ability to "sell" an idea or position;
- the ability to develop strategy;
- the ability to take on multiple tasks (handle multiple clients and issues and juggle priorities);
- knowledge of the specific area of law that pertains to your issue (especially if you need legal counsel in regard to the issue);
- time to devote to your project;
- hands-on style of getting in the trenches and walking the halls of the Capitol;
- ability to build and work with coalitions;
- no conflicts of interest with your issue or your organization;
- a top-notch reputation (respected by peers, legislators, and staff); and
- good judgment.

The Interview

Once you have identified a pool of lobbyists to consider based on research and referrals, contact the lobbyists to obtain background information on their firm, clear questions about conflicts of interest, and determine whether they are interested in and have the time to work with your association. After reviewing printed materials, schedule interviews. Some guidelines for the interview process are as follows:

- When possible, interview the candidates in person and in their office.

- Consider including your president and/or the government affairs committee chairperson to get "buy-in" from your leadership.

- Start the interview with an open-ended question, asking about their firm and its position on lobbying. Should something come out in their opening comments that doesn't feel right, don't be afraid to cut the interview short.

- Describe your organization and bring along the annual report, brochures, etc. Explain your issue and your objective thoroughly. Outline the resources you have available to assist them in accomplishing your goal. Tell them who the opponents will be and what their arguments will be.

- Explain the reporting system you want between yourself and the lobbyist; be sure to include such factors as whether you want oral or written reports (or both) and what you expect in terms of frequency of reports.

- Discuss the terms of the contract. Make clear the time commitment you expect from them (i.e., legislative sessions only, month-to-month, calendar year, or special sessions). Make clear the services and coverage you are looking for (legislative tracking and analysis only, or advocacy, too; only legislative coverage, or regulatory coverage, too; for a single issue or bill, or for general representation).

- Obtain references—these can be current clients, legislators, or even other lobbyists.

- Ask lobbyists for an assessment of your chances of success and an assessment of their suitability for the project. Lobbyists may say they can do everything, but there is no such thing as a sure win. Ask them to identify the weaknesses in your position; their answer can give you some valuable insights on how you are perceived. However, don't expect lobbyists to provide you with a full strategy in the interview process.

- It is neither fair nor appropriate to expect them to give away their trade secrets, and if you push them to do so and do not hire them, it could come back to haunt you. State capitals are very small communities.

- Notify all other candidates you have interviewed when you have made your final selection.

Evaluating Lobbyist Candidates— Other Things to Take into Consideration

Lobbyists should be evaluated in light of the previously mentioned characteristics. It is important that lobbyists be politically well-connected. Do they know the players and know them well? Make sure they can walk both sides of the aisle or, if not, that they have a team-mate who can cover the other side for them. They should have good relationships with key committee members and chairs and with the opposition, agency staff, and the governor's office. Their credibility and their track record should be strong.

Some things to keep in mind include the following:

- The most expensive and most well-known lobbyists won't necessarily be the right ones for your job.

- Consider the lobbyist's popularity amongst other lobbyists. The lobbying business is like a small fraternity; if your lobbyist is popular, the other lobbyists will help out.

- Do not be fooled into thinking your lobbyist must be a former office holder or have one working for the firm.

- If you hire a firm, know whom you are getting. You may interview the head of the firm, but the actual job may be assigned to a junior associate.

- Beware of "cause" lobbyists, who tend to be one-issue crusaders.

- Consider the image the lobbyist projects.

- If a lobbyist will be actively working your side of the issue on behalf of another client, go elsewhere and add to the work force in favor of your position rather than paying that lobbyist twice to weigh in on the same side of the issue.

- Don't worry too much about substantive expertise; while it is clearly a plus, remember that you must be the technical expert.

Marcie M. McNelis,
CAE

The Art of the Deal: Fee Negotiations

Completing a deal is very much a part of the process of choosing a lobbyist. First you must review the scope of the project with the lobbyist you have selected, again outlining your expectations. Establish goals. Will the lobbyist be covering only one issue, or all issues that surface? Will representation be legislative and regulatory, or legislative only? If you are contracting for single-issue work versus comprehensive representation, you may end up renegotiating. However, representation on all issues can make it more difficult to establish a fair fee and will cost more than restricting your project to a single issue. Do your best to evaluate and anticipate.

Next, request a fee proposal from the lobbyist. Be aware that hiring on a contingency basis on legislative issues is illegal in most states and in Congress. Contingency fee lobbying frequently is illegal on regulatory issues as well.

Hourly fees offer the wrong incentive, and no matter what your budget is, it probably will not be enough. You want your issue resolved as quickly and painlessly as possible. Request a flat fee.

Remember that fees vary widely from state to state; for example, California, Texas, Florida, and Michigan tend to be expensive states in which to lobby, while Maine, New Mexico, and Utah are much less costly.

Fees may also depend on your issue from state to state. For example, the predisposition of the legislature toward your issue or its legislative history in a particular state may make it more or less difficult to succeed. This will play into the cost.

The reputation of the individual or firm will affect cost as well. Some firms can demand large fees because of particularly strong contacts, track records, or expertise, and they probably are well worth it when you have a tough issue. It is important to match your needs and resources to achieve the right fit. You do not need the biggest name in town to provide background monitoring or to handle a minor issue on a defensive basis.

The next item to consider is expenses. You definitely should cover them because activity that requires out-of-pocket expenses (within lobbying and campaign law guidelines) generally contributes to the success of your project and facilitates good communication with you and with legislators. However, this coverage should not be open-ended. Consider a cap on the total, and insist on prior approval for expenses over a certain amount. Also budget for sales tax on lobbying services in those states where it is assessed (Connecticut, Hawaii, Iowa, Pennsylvania, South Dakota, and Vermont).

Finally, prepare a contract or letter of agreement that includes all pertinent aspects of the assignment. Your document should include the following:

- names of your point persons;

- objective/statement of work (avoid putting details of strategy—in the event the document could get in the hands of outsiders, do not put anything in writing that you would not want to read in the paper tomorrow);

- fee amount, payment schedule, and expense reimbursement policy;

- duration of contract;

- reporting requirements; and

- termination clause with notice requirements specified. (Note: terminating a lobbyists' contract during the legislative session in

Connecticut is illegal under the state's lobbying laws, because it is construed to be tied to contingent lobbying. Know the law.)

Once Hiring Is Done: Manage Your Lobbyist

Managing lobbyists is not much different from managing any other employees. You must spend some time with them. Provide a thorough orientation of both your organization and the issues. Have the lobbyists attend your government affairs committee meetings. Provide them with a thorough understanding of your issues and your positions. They will need to negotiate on your behalf, and you may not be present when these negotiations are taking place, so they need to know both your ideal and your fall-back positions. Make it clear, however, that consultation is expected when you have a change in strategy.

When your lobbyist meets with legislators and staff, meet with them also if you can. When you are making campaign contributions, deliver the check in person with the lobbyist (or send someone from your association) and go to lunches and fund-raisers, so credit does not go only to the lobbyist. Provide expert witnesses for hearings, and turn out local members to attend these hearings as well.

Be accessible, and have a backup person available when you are not able to be reached. Check in regularly—let the lobbyist know that you are on top of things, but do not micromanage the lobbyist.

Support your lobbyist with important resources—strong policy and factual arguments, legal issues, grassroots mobilization, quality member contacts who are constituents of pivotal legislators, public relations support, up-to-date statistics on the importance of your association's members in that jurisdiction (number of members and/or their employees in the state/district, tax dollars they contribute, economic development opportunities represented by bringing your members' business to the state, civic involvement of your organization and your members, local political involvement by members, etc.), expert witnesses, public opinion polls, political action committee funds, and members willing to volunteer on political campaigns and provide other in-kind contributions.

If you are looking for tax breaks, provide accurate statistics on the fiscal impact and suggestions for revenue replacement. If you have potential allies on the issue, be sure to identify these to the lobbyist and help the lobbyist enlist their support.

Develop goals, and make sure these are tangible. Set up milestones for a long-range strategy review. Provide for mid-course corrections,

Marcie M. McNelis, CAE

because you will invariably come across a detour at some point. Every lobbying campaign does.

Establish a reporting system. Telephone calls between you and the lobbyist may need to be made as often as every day, or only weekly. Others prefer to be called only when something happens. Written reports can be weekly, monthly, or just at the end of session. Most important, be clear about your expectations. Make sure your lobbyist is reporting to one person only—you should be responsible for getting information out to a broader audience, if need be.

To manage your lobbyist most effectively, remember you must be a part of the lobbying process. His or her role is that of the quarterback, your role is that of the coach.

The Evaluation Process

Evaluate a lobbyist in much the same way you do an employee. Review all aspects of the assignment: did they win, and if so, were they able to do so without creating any long-term harm or ill-will toward your association; were timely and thorough reports submitted; were they responsive to you; did they have the proper professional attitude; and did you receive their best effort? With this evaluation, you may make an informed decision as to whether or not to renew the contract. If you have made a good hiring decision in the first place, chances are you will not face performance problems that cannot be resolved.

If you decide to terminate the contract or not renew it, do so in a professional manner and in accordance with the provisions of the contract. Where possible, avoid the need to terminate the lobbyist. Remember that this can be dangerous, especially if the contract has not yet expired. Rather than firing the lobbyist, try to make it work and examine what responsibility you may have to bear for the difficulties you experienced. Discuss your dissatisfaction openly and honestly with the lobbyist and give him or her an opportunity to respond and to improve, just as you would an employee. If you decide to let the lobbyist go, remember these points:

- Don't bad-mouth the lobbyist, or give the lobbyist reason to bad-mouth you. It is not wise to make enemies out of lobbyists.

- Consider how you would handle the situation if the lobbyist were a regular employee, and then handle the situation even more carefully.

• Try to find a face-saving, but honest, rationale for letting the lobbyist go (e.g., your needs or objectives have changed, your budget has changed, the make-up of the legislature is changing or there will be a change in legislative leadership, your styles are too different, you are going to concentrate your resources elsewhere). If your issues allow, help the lobbyist save face by skipping representation in that state for a year, then start fresh the following year.

Conclusion

Hiring the right contract lobbyist can be a cost-effective and efficient way to achieve your legislative and regulatory objectives. It requires finding the right mix of good people skills, ability to communicate, experience, contacts, and perseverance.

Lobbying is a process, not an event. You must keep the pressure on. The most consistent, effective way to do this is to have a professional on the ground day in and day out in the capital.

Marcie M. McNelis, CAE

CHAPTER 7

Winning with Grassroots

John M. Sharbaugh, CAE

What Is a Grassroots Network?

In today's association government relations vernacular, "grassroots" refers to a grassroots network or program. A grassroots network may be defined as "an on-going, organized system of recruiting, training, and motivating members to use their political power to influence legislation." This definition offers some key points to understanding what is necessary for a successful grassroots network.

First, a successful grassroots network doesn't just happen, and it isn't ad hoc. Rather, it is a systematic program that must be developed and maintained for the duration of the association's government relations efforts. If you are just starting a grassroots network, you need to develop a well-thought-out plan to get it off the ground and then continually maintain it in good working order.

Although some of your members may volunteer their services to your grassroots network, you need to actively recruit to get both the quantity and quality of people you need to be successful.

Like any "army," don't assume the troops know what to do or will always want to do what needs to be done. You have to train your grassroots participants so they understand how the political process works and how they can be effective activists in that process. They need to understand the legislative and regulatory issues your association is facing so they can communicate effectively on them with legislators. Just as important, they need to be properly motivated to understand the importance of the role they play and that they can make a difference as an individual in the process.

Assembling the troops (your grassroots network) isn't enough. You need to ensure that they are properly prepared and outfitted to do the job.

The bottom line of any grassroots network is to influence the legislative process for the benefit of your association's members. That is the standard against which any program should be measured. If your network doesn't provide legislative results, it isn't working effectively, and you need to reexamine its operation. All grassroots networks should have some means for monitoring effectiveness. Although you cannot win every legislative battle, with an effective grassroots network you should win more than you lose.

John M. Sharbaugh, CAE

Why Is a Grassroots Network Important to Your Association?

The importance and power of grassroots political action has never been greater. Association government relations programs must incorporate an effective grassroots component if they are to be successful. Although professional legislative staff (lobbyists), political action committees (PACs), position papers, and media campaigns also are important facets of an effective government relations program, none of them can replace the power of constituents—people who vote—and their effect on elected officials.

Grassroots activity has always played a role in association government relations. However, since the mid-1970s several major shifts have occurred in the way political decisions are made that increase the importance of grassroots action and require associations to rethink strategies for conducting legislative affairs.

Some of these political changes include the following:

• The legislative and regulatory issues that affect associations and their members have grown at all levels of government in the past twenty years. This growing government activism correlates with growing government and legislative staffs. It is exacerbated by increased pressure to maintain existing government programs, while reducing or maintaining government budgets.

• The explosion in the number of PACs and the cost of political campaigns, combined with limitations on PAC spending, makes it critical to stand out from the crowd. To be effective, financial contributions must be combined with people power or people contributions.

- Interest groups have proliferated, as have their means of influencing legislators. Thus, there are now more participants than ever in the political process.

- The operation of Congress and many state legislatures has changed. The seniority system and party discipline are much less important today. The many subcommittees in Congress give nearly every member of Congress a public platform. Legislators have become more sophisticated and more independent. They no longer automatically look to their party or committee leadership for direction on issues.

- The introduction of term limits in many states ensures a constant turnover in the composition of legislatures, making it even more important to have strong constituent communications.

As a result of these changes, grassroots activity and the opinions of constituents have become increasingly important in the legislative process. One critical consideration for legislators is the perspective of their states or districts. Hearing from "back home" is, in most cases, more effective than hearing from a lobbyist in the Capitol. For these reasons, associations should establish a grassroots network to harness the political power of their members.

Support from Leadership

A successful association grassroots program must have the active and vocal support of association leaders—both volunteer and staff. This support can be demonstrated, in part, by allocating adequate resources (financial and human) to get the job done. It also includes continuous vocal and visible reminders from leadership to the members. The membership must be constantly told by leadership why grassroots activity is important and why it is critical to the organization's legislative success.

If the association's leadership is not committed to the cause, if leaders are not willing to provide the necessary resources, and if they do not sincerely believe in the necessity and appropriateness of political activity and involvement, the program is doomed to failure or—at best—limited success. Commitment starts from the top down. Before you do anything else, make sure you have the necessary commitment of association leadership to ensure the success of your grassroots program.

Types of Grassroots Networks

Generally speaking, grassroots networks fall into one of two categories: quantitative or qualitative.

A quantitative or broad-based network emphasizes getting as many participants as possible into the program. Associations that use this approach seek to involve as many members as they can who are willing to call or write their legislators, regardless of their firsthand knowledge or relationship with the elected official. All members are welcomed into the program. The key element is their willingness to communicate with the elected official when asked. Generally, participants receive regular newsletters on legislative matters and occasionally action alerts or calls to action on specific legislative issues.

John M. Sharbaugh,
CAE

Qualitative grassroots networks, often called "key person" programs, place greater emphasis on the quality of the relationship between a participant and a legislator. Rather than focusing on large numbers of participants, the goal of this type of program is to establish high-quality personal relationships between at least one association member and each legislator. These programs are not necessarily restricted to one member per legislator; in some cases, several members may have an excellent relationship with a particular legislator. In a key person program, the critical element is the relationship between an association member or members and the elected official. Communications between the members and legislators take place on an on-going basis. Personal relationships with the legislator and his or her staff are cultivated. Thus, when there is a need to communicate on a particular legislative issue, there is greater receptivity and response from the legislator.

Some associations may use a combination of these two approaches, or they may be in a transition—moving from a quantitative to a qualitative program. Generally, a qualitative approach provides better results than a quantitative approach unless the organization has an extremely large number of members that can generate an avalanche of mail or calls to elected officials.

Members of Congress now receive volumes of mail each year. The House and Senate post offices indicated that they processed over 38 million pieces of mail in 1997. Thus, close and personal relationships, meetings, and communications have a greater effect on today's political leaders. Letters and calls from constituents that legislators know and trust will have the greatest effect for an association.

Third-Party Programs

Although the primary participants of an association's grassroots network generally are members of the organization, there may be times when it is appropriate and strategically sound to use external constituencies in the lobbying effort on a specific legislative issue. Expanding your grassroots efforts to groups outside the association can help position the issue as one that has a broad reach that affects a large number of voters and can provide a larger base of constituents to help lobby legislators.

One way to do this is to approach other organized groups or associations that may have an interest in the legislative issue of concern. Working in a coalition with other groups can provide a multiplier effect for your lobbying effort.

Another option is to generate support from the population at large by identifying individuals who may have a personal interest in the particular legislative issue. A political consulting or grassroots firm that specializes in this area may be helpful. Although this approach can be expensive, it may be worth it if the issue is serious and it is important to position the issue as one of broad general concern to generate legislative support. Be sure the services of the grassroots consulting firm include some type of tracking or verification process to ensure that the results are being achieved through actual contacts with legislators.

The greatest risk in expanding your grassroots activity outside your membership base is the loss of control of managing the activity. Also, other groups may not have the same commitment or level of interest in the issue. It is important to keep this in mind before pursuing any third-party activity. In any coalition effort, it is important to make sure you are one of the key players in managing the overall process to ensure that your interests are protected.

Identifying and Recruiting Participants

Another essential element of an association grassroots program is identifying and recruiting members to participate in the program. Any and all sources of recruitment should be considered. If you are running a quantitative program, you are looking for all the warm bodies you can muster. In a qualitative program, you should identify members who already have a relationship with an elected official. But members who are willing to establish a relationship should not be overlooked. Members who are motivated can be taught how to develop and nurture a close constituent relationship.

There are several ways to identify and recruit your grassroots network, including the following:

- Run articles and notices in various association publications.
- Make pitches at various association meetings.
- Use state affiliate groups or chapters to help identify people.
- Talk with legislators and their staffs to see what members of your group they may already know—then recruit those members.
- Review Federal Election Commission reports to identify members who have contributed to campaigns—then recruit those members.

The key is to ask people to join. Don't wait for people to come to you. Every association has members who are willing to participate or who already have relationships with elected officials, but many will not volunteer. They will help only if they are asked.

John M. Sharbaugh, CAE

Training

Whatever grassroots approach an association selects, it is important to train the participants so that they understand essential elements, including:

- the overall goals of the association's government relations program;
- their role in the program and why it is important;
- how the legislative process really works;
- how they can develop and maintain effective relationships with legislators and their staffs;
- how they can communicate effectively with elected officials;
- the importance of legislative staff; and
- the major legislative issues of the day affecting the association's members.

Training can be provided through various formats, including national or regional conferences, state conferences or seminars, and programs at the local level. For its national or regional conference, a national association can select speakers and program content aimed at training. This sort of conference probably will be inexpensive for the association; however, the number of people reached is likely to be small.

The reverse is true, on a proportional basis, with state or local programs. The more localized the training effort is, the more people you will probably reach. The challenge is to provide a high-quality program on a cost-effective basis—ensuring the quality of speakers and content.

One option is to develop a packaged training program that can be used by state and local groups in a variety of formats. By developing training materials, discussion leader guides, and video tapes, the association can ensure a consistent message and quality program. This approach helps the organization to reach the most people cost effectively.

This approach requires a cooperative effort with an association's state or local chapters or state affiliate groups. Although such a cooperative effort can be challenging, its rewards are high. It provides a means of "spreading the gospel" of grassroots involvement to the largest possible audience over a long period of time. Once the program is developed, its "shelf life" should be indeterminate—because the principles taught are unlikely to change frequently. This approach helps to build a relationship with state and local groups and helps generate the mind-set that grassroots activity is important and is everybody's business.

To develop a packaged training program, some associations hire political consultants with experience in this field. The materials developed—written and videotaped—should be high quality to ensure their acceptance and use by state and local groups. If your association does not have this type of expertise on staff, it is wise to outsource some of this activity to a known political affairs expert.

Another critical component of a grassroots training program is adequate training of discussion leaders, to teach them how to use the materials. Training for discussion leaders can be held on a national, regional, or local level. This type of training can help to recruit and motivate leaders who will execute the program in the field.

Communications with Members Is Critical

Once your association has developed its basic grassroots network—that is, you have identified and recruited your participants and put them through some basic training—it is important that you have regular and effective communications with them. Effective communications helps keep members of your network informed and motivated and connected to the program. It's also necessary to help members carry out their role of regular communications with legislators.

There are several ways to carry out this communication with your members. They include the following:

Newsletters. A regular newsletter to your grassroots participants can help keep them up to date on legislative activities and issues. It's also a tangible way to make them feel connected to and part of a special program. Producing a newsletter requires some resources, but with today's technology, investment can be minimal. The most difficult part will be finding articles for your newsletter. Generally, there are always legislative issues to cover. You also can provide participants with general tips and reminders on how to be effective in the political process. A regular newsletter also provides an effective vehicle to highlight legislative success and members who have performed well in their grassroots role for the association.

John M. Sharbaugh, CAE

Position Papers. Position papers on specific legislative issues can be a useful supplement to the newsletters. Position papers should explain the issue of concern in detail to ensure that members understand the issue and how it affects them and their association. Position papers can be used to advise your members about the opinions and positions of any opposition on your legislative issues so they are prepared to deal with it should it arise in conversations with legislators.

Fax. Faxes can provide an easy and quick way to communicate with members and deliver information, such as newsletters and position papers. You should ask your network members how they prefer to receive their newsletters and position papers. Although most people will want to receive things by fax, some may not or cannot.

Internet/Web Site. The Internet is another fast and inexpensive way to communicate with members. Although the Internet is not yet used as often as the fax, use of the Internet is growing. Again, poll the members of your network first about their desired information delivery mode.

Your association's Web site, if your association has one, is another good place to put information about government relations issues. Make sure members know how to access the information, and make the process as user friendly as possible. Also, consider the sensitivity of the information you put on your Web site. You may want to have certain information concerning your legislative strategy protected so only members can access it.

Toll-free Telephone Numbers. Another option is to provide members with a toll-free telephone number to call to hear recorded updates on recent legislative activity. This is an easy way for members to stay informed. It requires periodically updating the recorded information and installing and using a separate phone line.

Staff Calls. Calling network members periodically promotes a "personal touch." It gives you an opportunity to update them on recent legislative activities and to answer any questions they may have. These calls will give members a feeling that they are an important part of your program. You also can obtain current information from them about any meetings they have had with legislators in their districts.

The key to effective communications is to ensure that you communicate with the members of your network on a regular basis. You may choose to use all or some of the methods described above, or you may have some other options. What's important is that you communicate somehow and that you do it often enough to provide members with an understanding of your issues and their importance in your efforts. If you communicate with your members only when there is a problem, they are not going to feel motivated to respond and will not be properly prepared.

Action Alerts

Effective ongoing communication pays off when you need your grass-roots network to take action regarding a particular piece of legislation that is being acted on or considered in the state legislature or Congress. In this situation, many associations use a "call to action" or "action alert" that gives members specific instructions to contact particular legislators about a particular legislative bill or amendment.

Action alerts usually are extremely time-sensitive communications because of the nature of the legislative process. Often, the time frame for response is extremely limited, and it is critical that your grass-roots network respond immediately if your association's message is going to be heard by legislators and help provide the desired result.

To ensure timely response to action alerts by your members, make sure you carry out the functions described earlier in this chapter—that is, effectively recruiting and training members and providing them with regular communications about your issues and the importance of their role as grassroots activists. If you have done these things well, your members will be ready and willing to respond when they get an action alert.

The information you provide in your action alert also can help to get the type of response you want and need from your members. First, keep the alert as concise and to the point as possible. Do not overwhelm your members with paper. This will discourage them from reading the material. Describe the specific issue or concern, why it is important, and what you want them to communicate to legislators. Make sure they know they can call you if they want more details or if they have questions, but keep the written material you send them to a minimum.

Make it clear to them how they should communicate with their assigned legislator. If the situation is extremely time sensitive, their only option will be to make a phone call. If more time is available, they can write a letter or arrange to meet with the legislator when he or she is back home in the district. Make sure your members understand how you want them to carry out the communication process and how much time they have to do so.

Action alerts should be issued sparingly. They should be issued in only the most critical situations to help pass or defeat a specific legislative proposal. If their use becomes routine, their effectiveness will diminish with your members who will tire of responding. Frequent alerts also may have a negative effect on legislators who are constantly receiving calls or letters from your members.

Timing is critical when using action alerts. If you send action alerts too soon, the message your members deliver may get lost before legislators are focused on the particular issue. If you send the alerts too late, your message may not arrive in time to affect the vote or outcome of the issue. As a government relations professional, you need to learn how to manage this action alert process effectively and strategically to complement your other lobbying efforts.

Finally, it is important that you have a feedback mechanism built into your action alert process. You need to know whether your members actually carried out the communications with legislators. A response form should be provided for them to tell you with whom they communicated, what was the response or reaction (i.e., will they support or oppose the bill), and if there is anything you can do to follow up with additional information.

You may want to call members to find out what action they have taken and the response they have received. This will give you a chance to ask additional questions and get more details. It also will help reinforce for your members the fact that you are monitoring the issue and care about what they are doing.

John M. Sharbaugh, CAE

Other Projects for Grassroots Activists

There are other ways your members can develop or enhance their relationships with legislators. You should ensure that your members are familiar with their legislators and encourage their participation.

Attend Town Hall Meetings

Many legislators hold town hall meetings in their districts. You should encourage your members to attend these events to help them better understand the issues of concern to their legislator. It is also a way for them to make themselves known to the legislator and his or her staff.

Host a Business Site Tour or Special Event

Inviting your legislator to tour your business or firm or attend a special event, such as a dinner, can help members enhance their relationship, especially if it provides exposure to other constituents in the legislator's district. This is a good public relations opportunity for the legislator, and it is an opportunity for members to explain their business and community involvement and the issues that concern them.

Careful planning for the legislator's visit is important. Some key points for your members to remember include the following:

- Members should send a written invitation to the legislator. They shouldn't be discouraged if several invitations are declined before one is accepted. Legislators have many demands on the time they spend in the district or state. Persistence will pay off.

- Members should develop a schedule that allows enough time for the visit or special event and for informal discussion, which is important. If the legislator's schedule permits, they should plan a small luncheon preceding, during, or following a visit.

- Members should find out who will accompany the legislator or encourage the legislator to bring the district representative or a key aide. They should make transportation arrangements for them, if necessary.

- Members should make sure they share information about their business or group the legislator might want to know (e.g., the size of their firm, the number and nature of customers they serve, community or philanthropic projects in which they may be involved, and the kinds of specialized services they provide).

- Members should send a thank-you note to the legislator after the visit.

- If photos were taken during the visit, copies should be sent to the legislator.

Organize an Advisory Group

A legislator may be receptive to working with an informal advisory group of constituents in the district or state that can provide advice on issues affecting their particular industry. Members might work with their legislator to organize this group. The goal should be to cultivate this arrangement, so that the legislator will turn to them for advice on issues that affect their business or industry, as well as for insights on the local community and economy. Their legislator will be better informed, and they will have ongoing opportunities to develop a closer relationship.

Keep the following points in mind:

- Include in the advisory group people who have different areas of expertise and interests and who have expressed a willingness to work with the legislator.

- Limit the size of the group. If an advisory group covers a district, you may need no more than three or four people.

- Plan to meet with the legislator two or three times a year in an informal setting.

- Keep the meeting format simple, and invite freewheeling discussion. Choose a variety of topics and issues to address.

- Be sensitive to the legislator's time, and schedule the length of meetings accordingly.

- Send the legislator and each participant thank-you letters and a summary of the key points of the discussions.

Host a Fund-raiser

An effective and simple way for members to develop a personal relationship with a legislator, or a potential legislator, is to host a candidate fund-raiser. Hosting a fund-raiser also will help members establish themselves as key players in the politics of their district.

There are a wide variety of fund-raisers members could sponsor or host. At least initially, however, the best approach may be to conduct a fund-raiser in their home. This approach gives members the opportunity to make the fund-raiser personal and intimate, and thus foster a closer relationship with the candidate. Second, a fund-raiser in their home will have more of an impact on the candidate. As a guest in a home, the legislator or candidate will have the opportunity to meet and speak with dozens of potential voters.

Volunteer in a Campaign

Members can make a valuable contribution to their legislator's reelection efforts by volunteering to work in the campaign. There are dozens of ways in which volunteers are used, including working in phone banks, serving on the finance committee, putting up yard signs, doing candidate and issue research, canvassing neighborhoods, handing out literature on election day, and so forth.

Members may call the candidate or the volunteer coordinator of the campaign to volunteer their services. They should not be discouraged if they are not immediately successful in getting plugged into the campaign. Campaigns tend to be chaotic and disorganized. Persistence will pay off.

Communications with Legislators

Members should understand how to properly communicate with legislators. Primary communications methods are in person, by phone, and in writing.

Personal Visits

Legislators are busy people, so members should make an appointment to meet with legislators to discuss a specific issue. Many legislators will make every effort to meet with constituents, particularly if the constituent has traveled to make the meeting.

It is not unusual, however, for legislative schedules to change unexpectedly. In such instances, many legislators will try to at least greet the visitor, talk with him or her for a few moments, and then ask the visitor to meet with an appropriate staff person. They may also try to reschedule the appointment or arrange a time for a phone conversation. Members should be prepared for these schedule changes and be as flexible as possible. If they are unable to meet with the legislator, they should take advantage of the opportunity to become acquainted with or solidify their relationship with the legislator's staff.

Some things members should remember when communicating with legislators or their staff include the following:

Don't assume you have to press, or discuss, your issues every time you talk with your legislator. One of the quickest ways a grassroots activist can reduce his or her effectiveness is by becoming a nuisance. Don't communicate with your legislator only when you want something, and don't wear him or her out by discussing your industry-specific issues every time you are together or talk by telephone. Discuss things that are of interest and importance to the legislator. Save arguments and views on your issues until you feel the situation is appropriate for presenting them or unless it is at the specific request of the legislator or in response to an action alert from your association.

John M. Sharbaugh,
CAE

Offer to serve as a resource person for the legislators and their staff on your industry's issues. Legislators often are confronted with complex, technical issues that they must understand and address. Their staff often must gather information on the subject to be used to reach a final decision. Members should offer to help in this area; doing so can pay dividends in terms of enhancing their relationship with the legislator and staff.

There are some general principles that can apply to any contact your members make with their legislator on any issue.

Be prepared. Members should do their homework ahead of time and know exactly what they are going to discuss and all the points they want to cover. They should anticipate other issues or questions the legislator may raise that are related to their topic. They already should be familiar with the legislator's background, perspective on issues, other legislative interests, and so forth. They should consider these when preparing for their visit and try to approach the issue from a perspective that will appeal to the legislator.

Establish a common denominator. Members should set the stage at the beginning of their conversation with the legislator by reinforcing some common ground. This will vary from legislator to legislator. Members may be able to refer to agreement on the substance of an issue or thank the legislator for a recent vote on which he or she supported your interests. You may be able to refer to some common interests, acquaintances, or activities in the district. It is important for members to take advantage of any previous incident that reinforces commonality or agreement—without being insincere.

Be concise, specific, and clear. After the members' opening conversation, they should refer to the purpose of their visit. Members' meetings with legislators will vary in length, but the typical meeting is about a half-hour long. Maximizing this time requires that members be as clear, concise, and specific as possible. If members are asking the legislator to take a specific action involving a specific topic at a specific time, they should give him or her all the details.

Requests for action can take many forms, such as voting for or against a bill, supporting or opposing amendments or substitutions, generating support among other legislators, signing "Dear Colleague" letters, making speeches on the floor of the House or Senate, cosponsoring a piece of legislation, or inserting items in the record. If members are meeting to relate background information and discuss the association's analysis on an issue that will require action in the future, they should be clear about that, too; they should assure the legislator of their willingness to keep him or her updated and to discuss the matter again when the specific strategy is identified.

Be reasonable. Members should not overstate their case, or they risk losing credibility. Members should use factual information and concrete real-life examples, as much as possible, to support their viewpoint. They should not deliver ultimatums or be argumentative. If the legislator's perspective differs from the members', members should listen to the legislator's comments but should not be dissuaded from making their own points.

Members should not make commitments on behalf of the association to lend support or opposition to issues on which it has taken no position. Only personal assurances of support or commitments to explore the legislator's suggestions on issues are appropriate.

Members should not embarrass the legislator by assuming that he or she is familiar with the details of the issue they are discussing. Legislators must deal with many complex issues. It is impossible for them to be thoroughly updated on all of them, so they tend to concentrate on those areas of personal interest or areas that fall under the jurisdiction of the committees on which they sit. They rely heavily on staff to keep them informed.

Localize (humanize) the issue. Legislators deal with many issues from a broad, national perspective. They can lose sight of how a legislative proposal will affect the daily lives of their constituents back in the state or district. Members can help bridge that gap for their legislators by giving them examples of how a particular proposal will affect the lives of their constituents—either positively or negatively. Members should humanize the issue so that legislators can see beyond national or state cost figures or national or state averages.

Acknowledge the opposition. But don't denigrate them. Members should mention the arguments being used by the opposition and address them. Legislators recognize that every issue has at least two sides. By responding to the opponents' statements, members demonstrate their depth of understanding and, perhaps, neutralize the opposition's influence.

Provide written materials. Members should leave the legislator and/or the appropriate staff their business card and a brief summary of the issue they have just discussed. Members may choose to also leave any lengthier resource documents that have additional data reinforcing their position statements. This type of information should be provided by the association.

Close the sale. Members should ask legislators if they can count on the legislators' support. Members need to know where the legislators stand, and it is not unreasonable to expect them to advise the member of their position.

Say thank you. Legislators appreciate recognition, encouragement, and thanks. Members should take every appropriate opportunity during and at the end of their visit to express these sentiments.

Follow up promptly. Members should send a letter to legislators immediately after the meeting to thank them for their time and attention and to briefly summarize the content and nature of the discussion. Thank them in advance for any assistance or support they have offered. If legislators were noncommittal during the meeting, members should assure them of their willingness to answer questions or provide additional information.

Members should include any written materials that they had promised to send during the meeting. Members should remind legislators of the presence of the association's office and of the availability of its resources and personnel. Members should send a copy of the letter to their association.

Report immediately. Members should contact their association immediately after the meeting. Members' comments are valuable in determining the extent and nature of the follow-up that will be required by association staff in their daily activities.

The members' report should include a description of the general tenor of the conversation; exactly who they spoke to; if there were any staff participating along with the legislator or if they met only with staff; whether or not the legislator made a commitment to their request for action and the reasons for either decision; and their assessment of follow-up required and the role played by staffers, if any were present.

Phone Contact

There may be many times when your members' contact with a legislator will be conducted by phone. Important committee mark-ups of legislation, floor votes, or conference sessions sometimes are scheduled abruptly and are subject to last-minute changes. The dynamics of issues can shift, compelling changes in strategy. When these situations preclude the possibility of a personal visit with the legislator or his or her staff, phone conversation is the next best option.

If members already have a good relationship with legislators or their staff, their chances of getting through to legislators directly and quickly, or of legislators returning their call quickly, are vastly improved. In some cases, the legislator may ask a staff person to return the call. If timing is critical, this may be the only opportunity to impart your message. In any case, members should give the full benefit of their comments to the staff person. If it is still essential to speak directly to the legislator, members should express their desire to do so—courteously—and ask if there is a convenient time when they can call back or be available for the legislator to call them.

The same checklist for personal contacts also applies to phone contacts—with particular emphasis on the need to be clear, concise, and specific. It is also critical that members report the results of their phone conversation to the association immediately.

Written Comments

There are several circumstances when written comments by members will be both necessary and appropriate. Some of these include the following:

- follow-up to a personal visit to thank a legislator for his or her commitment to take a specific action;
- thank-you letters for specific actions taken;

- follow-up to a personal visit to reaffirm the association's position and arguments for a legislator who has been noncommittal on an issue or action the member requested;
- supplementation of personal contacts, when the overall legislative strategy calls for legislators to receive a volume of mail on a particular issue;
- letters to relay background or resource information that will be of help or interest to the legislator or that will assist in building a positive climate;
- personal notes to relay items of interest in the district; and
- when timing is critical and phone contact has been impossible.

John M. Sharbaugh, CAE

In all cases, written communications should adhere to the same guidelines as personal contacts—with some additional suggestions. Whenever possible, letters should be written on the members' own stationery and in their own words.

The association should get copies of the members' correspondence and legislator's response.

Use of Faxes or E-mail

Although every legislator's office has a facsimile machine and many are able to receive electronic mail, it generally is not recommended that members send their personal communications in this way, unless the legislator or his or her staff specifically request it. Members should send their written material by mail or overnight delivery.

Reap the Benefits

Grassroots activity is essential for any association that wants to be successful in its legislative efforts. In today's political environment, the power of grassroots has never been greater and is likely to continue to grow in importance.

To succeed on the grassroots front, an association needs the commitment of its leadership to develop an effective grassroots network. Members must be educated as to the importance of the cause and recruited to be active participants in the network.

Associations with a meaningful grassroots network will reap the benefits in several ways. They experience greater legislative effectiveness, and they will enjoy a more active and committed membership. Finally, an effective grassroots network will enable your association to be viewed as a key player in helping shape public policy for the benefit of association members and the public.

CHAPTER 8

Expanding Your Clout through Coalitions

Pamela Phillips

COALITIONS OFTEN MAKE for strange but effective bedfellows. Yet many associations are reluctant to join forces with other organizations for a common purpose. Associations that are inexperienced in the art of evaluating and participating in coalitions fear they will lose their identity and fail to reach their true objectives by joining a coalition. In addition, when offered opportunities, these associations often feel hard pressed to decide which coalitions they should or should not join.

Benefits of Joining Coalitions

Joining a coalition offers many tangible and clear-cut benefits. First and most important, coalitions offer the power of numbers. An association with only 2,000 members may not, on its own, gain the attention of members of Congress on a particular priority issue. However, when this same organization joins forces with ten other organizations of similar size and views, 2,000 votes become 20,000 votes—a block of citizens too large to ignore.

Second, because coalitions bring together varying organizations, each interested in a different facet of the debate, they can offer a global viewpoint. A coalition's members can come from diverse groups that happen to agree on one issue. Diversity can help prevent certain groups in the coalition from appearing self-serving, because the coalition represents many participants on an issue, not just those who would directly benefit from the groups' advocacy position.

Coalitions can help an organization refine its arguments and strengthen its position. For example, interesting discussions among coalition members are likely to take place while the group is developing its position. These discussions could help to point out what legislative leaders and other organizations might think of the advocacy position.

Finally, coalitions offer each member organization the benefit of shared resources. This is particularly important for smaller associations, which may not have an overabundance of money, staff, legislative experience, and political contacts.

Once your organization understands the benefits of joining a coalition, the next step is to develop a series of objective criteria with which you can evaluate each coalition opportunity. The following are some areas to consider:

- **Driving Force**—Many coalitions are initiated and organized by one or more central organizations. Before you join a coalition, it is important to evaluate the driving-force organization and determine if you are comfortable with its lead position.

- **Coalition Goals**—What are the long- and short-range goals of this coalition? Are they exactly on point with what your organization hopes to accomplish or only similar? One good litmus test is to ask yourself: If this group accomplished everything in its mission statement, how would my board and membership feel?

- **Coalition Membership**—Almost as important as a coalition's goals and objectives is its membership. Are the group's members reputable and credible organizations with whom you would not mind sharing a reputation? Are they groups with which your association has worked before and found to be professional and cooperative?

- **Business Operations**—It is critical to understand how the coalition does business before you join. Issues such as prior approval of printed materials or allocation of votes are important to understand up front, so that you do not experience any surprises once you elect to become a member.

- **Resources**—What resources does the coalition have (i.e., dedicated staff, a meeting location, access to a lobbyist, etc.)? Because many coalitions require each member to support its operation in one way or another, it is critical that you determine what types of support in what amounts you will be expected to contribute.

• **Credibility**—If the coalition you are considering has been in existence for some time, or has operated previously under a different name on a different issue, what was and is its reputation with legislators and staff?

Your organization should understand that a majority of coalitions are temporary task forces that are intended to have both a limited scope and life span. If the coalition changes or if the criteria your association used to determine your affiliation change, it is critical for your association to know both how and when to leave a coalition.

If you or your membership becomes uncomfortable with any aspect of your relationship with the coalition, the first step is to meet with coalition leadership and determine if your concerns can be addressed. Administrative concerns, such as the coalition's business operations, may be modified without much controversy. However, if your concerns surround something substantive, such as how the coalition presents its message to elected officials or who the coalition elect to use as its spokespersons, the coalition may not be able to compromise.

If a compromise cannot be reached, you must determine whether your organization can remain a part of the coalition and still meet its own goals. If not, then ending your relationship with the coalition may be your only choice.

If you decide to leave a coalition, it is best to do so in a professional and honest manner. First, express your reasons for leaving both in writing and verbally to the coalition leaders, and ask that your comments be shared with the coalition membership. This helps to demonstrate what aspects of the coalition your organization may elect to support independently. In the end, fellow coalition members may work to develop a position that is more acceptable to your organization and that might gain more broad-based support on Capitol Hill or in a state capitol.

By leaving the coalition on a positive and open note, you leave the door open for future affiliations with any of the coalition members and you do not damage your organization's reputation by departing in anger.

How and when to join a coalition is as much instinctive as it is an objective decision. If your organization has limited resources and goals that may coincide with other organizations, coalitions might be just the public policy tool you need.

Permanent Coalitions

In chemistry, when distinct elements join to form a body, the result is called a molecule. In government affairs, the result is called a coalition. Like a molecule, a coalition can be temporary or permanent, depending on the purpose it serves.

Coalitions generally are formed by associations that share a common cause. In the case of a permanent coalition, the cause they hold in common is continuous and, most likely, is formed by associations within the same industry.

In a permanent coalition, you may find cross memberships. When major corporations are members of several associations within the coalition, these associations find themselves being asked to perform the same tasks. By forming a permanent coalition, associations can consolidate their obligations to fulfill these tasks through coalition staff. So a coalition should save you money through joint ventures that you would otherwise be forced to do alone. An exception is when the coalition is run primarily by one large association that is footing the bill for the smaller members.

A permanent coalition need not incorporate. It can be located within the offices of a coalition member, and for Internal Revenue Service purposes, coalition staff are employees of the host association. Financial contributions made by other coalition members are deposited in the account of the host association but segregated on the books from all other income and expense items.

A Model for One Large and Several Small Associations

Another model of a permanent coalition includes one large industry association that houses the coalition staff and picks up the bulk of the expenses. Smaller associations within the industry are brought in to enhance grassroots political strength and to give more significance to actions taken by the coalition. An example of this model is the Travel and Tourism Government Affairs Counsel, in Washington, D.C.

Regardless of which form of coalition suits your needs, a coalition should not replace the individual associations in the eyes of the industry; if this happens, the associations will begin to resent the coalition. Each association must gain credit from its members for work performed within the joint effort.

The following are some tips on how to manage a coalition effectively:

- Don't clutter the coalition agenda with unnecessary issues.

- Don't include issues on the agenda that could obtain a coalition consensus only in the event of an emergency.

- Don't waste valuable time on nuisance issues.

- Don't have the coalition become involved in an issue solely to allow your association to observe a rival association or group. You may be involved in a coalition with others you do not trust; but to be effective, integrity must be maintained.

- Coalitions, by nature, should adopt positions and take actions via unanimous consent. If you are continually protesting positions and actions taken by the coalition, you shouldn't be a member.

- Remember that the person directing the coalition must be seen at all times as a fair arbiter of conflicting interests. Although coalition members may agree on issue positions, discussions regarding potential actions can become quite heated, and impartiality can become difficult to maintain and present to members.

Be aware that member associations may drop out of temporary coalitions if their issues are resolved by legislators. They may get an offer that they can't refuse because it accommodates their industry. Those remaining within the coalition must accept their departure. Those leaving the coalition should not become public critics of their former allies. Although you can professionally accept an offer by elected officials to solve your industry problem, it would be unprofessional to turn around and become a critic of the organization in which you once participated.

Members of a permanent coalition, however, cannot drop out to cut a separate deal and cannot become a public critic of coalition activity.

In your communication activities, do not issue press releases on coalition letterhead unless everyone agrees with the statements made. Always ask why the coalition is sending out press releases in the name of member associations. It may be better to have the member associations sending out press releases using coalition data. Use coalition data and results to show members and the media the proactive stance of your association.

Truths and Axioms of Permanent Coalitions

1. A coalition must carefully and precisely define its goals and agenda, bearing in mind the often overlapping constituencies and competing goals of its members.

2. All coalition members must agree to the process by which positions are adopted.

3. A coalition will not be effective on any issue with which even one coalition member strongly disagrees.

4. In setting its agenda and in the long run, a coalition must avoid two extremes: dealing exclusively with issues that are too difficult or controversial for its members to undertake individually and focusing exclusively on issues that are too trivial for members to bother with on their own.

5. A coalition often plays a valuable role for certain members by adopting a position that reinforces or provides a broader ratification of a position that is of high priority to one or more of its members.

6. Although a coalition should let its members take maximum credit for its successes, two caveats apply: Members may want to use the coalition as a shield on certain issues, and it's sometimes necessary to recognize the coalition to enhance its overall credibility.

7. It is difficult (although not impossible) for a coalition to develop an effective grassroots network because its members may be reluctant to allow direct access to their constituents. The corollary here is that, for both legal and political reasons, coalitions are unlikely to develop effective political action committees.

8. As larger coalitions become more diffused in their objectives and agendas, they tend to develop "subcoalitions" to narrow the scope of mutual concerns and to focus on specific issues.

9. Frequent communication with members is critical for a coalition's success.

10. Coalition managers must preserve the trust of all coalition members, especially when positions they favor are not adopted by their coalitions or when sudden changes in coalition lobbying strategies or tactics are required.

11. Coalitions must be action-oriented, not merely information exchanges. They also should alert and educate their members about issues and topics of importance that might otherwise be overlooked.

12. Coalitions can perform a valuable role in defining the parameters of an industry.

Local Coalitions

Building coalitions for political action generally takes one of two forms: ongoing activities or special-purpose groups. Ongoing, permanent groups can be an important resource that allows you to expand in rapid response to any given issue. Permanent interface groups become the work force that, in turn, has the ability to identify additional resources to bring to bear on key issues that you, as a group, prioritize. The group can be a communication channel for candidate identification, response to ballot initiatives in their early stages, or any government agenda action item.

The ability to maintain an ongoing work group depends on the community size, the personalities and nature of your community players, and the nature of the issues you face. The coalition's willingness to allow participants to "agree to disagree" on some important issues can be critical to maintaining long-term relationships. However, it will be much easier to respond to a problem if you are already participating in a group that shares common values and goals.

When a key issue begins to evolve, the formation of an action-oriented group to achieve a special purpose becomes necessary. A good name, strong leadership, an effective strategy, and staffing and funding to implement that strategy are all important components to creating a new, effective coalition.

Coalitions Facing a Referendum

The first rule for coalitions that face an initiative or referendum is not to take the opponent for granted. There are several tools the campaign will need, but almost all of the tools require meaningful coalitions. To the extent that you have maintained your permanent coalition efforts, the job of creating a special-purpose initiative coalition will be simplified. The balance of this section will deal with tasks in creating and maintaining special-purpose coalitions.

Coalition Management

Volunteer leadership is one of the most difficult problems to address when creating and maintaining special-purpose coalitions. Begin with an executive or steering committee that, as a rule, consists of the people paying the bills (those individuals representing associations or private interests who will fund the campaign), particularly the start-up costs.

A steering committee can be helpful when you need to maintain the democratic participation of larger groups or constituencies, while also maintaining the executive committee to make and fund financial commitments. Large steering committees or coalition member meetings often become necessary to maintain morale in the face of strong grassroots opposition efforts. Otherwise, you may have to concede the "voice of the people" to your adversaries. It also becomes an effective way of giving a voice to coalition organizations that are not major funding sources.

During the process of fighting an initiative, do not give up on the need to obtain the endorsement or support of other community groups. To the extent that you can continue to bring them into your coalition (even when your polls show you have already won the election), you are building your strength for future issues. Continue to look to your existing database of voting patterns or polling responses to identify participants. Consider a direct-mail piece to solicit new participation in your new coalition and sell your message at the same time. Assess your media participants and how they may be used to solicit grassroots participants.

Coalitions to Defeat an Issue in Front of an Elective Body

It can be substantially easier to organize coalitions to defeat an issue before a legislative body than it is to effect the outcome of an election where you are essentially organizing a campaign. However, many of the fundamentals still apply: identify your participants, solicit leadership, organize a strategy, and sell that strategy and message to coalition members. Even in very large communities, 300 business representatives at a meeting speaking in opposition to ill-conceived legislation is an intimidating prospect to any elected official.

Media Communications

Building a relationship with the media can be difficult. Even paid professional media consultants can have a hard time selling the message of some groups. With the media, as with all coalitions, you will be seeking alternatives—ways to support good results or relationships and methods for dealing with poor results.

Begin with a list of the alternative means of communicating within your community. Reporting alternatives and opinions may include the following:

- **Newspaper Reporters.** Often, the reporter has a different perspective than does the editor.

- **Newspaper Editors.** Consider visiting editors regularly. Many papers have a policy for meeting with the editorial staff. If you can combine regular meetings with other business interests, they usually are receptive.

- **Alternative Papers.** Suburban, community papers or local newsletters can become a source of getting out information or initiating a story in the mainstream media.

- **Television.** Typically, more people watch television than read the paper. Know the stations in your market, and look for ways to reach their reporters and news directors. Reporters and news directors have much the same relationship as those of the editor/reporter discussed above. In regard to cable television, look for syndicated shows or alternative programming. Effective use of call-in shows can be made. It is also a good way to find people to drive messages not getting through in the mainstream media.

- **Direct Mail.** Begin your own newsletter or direct mail piece, even if it is only to attract mainstream media over the short term. Direct mail helps to carry the message directly to the populace; if the message is accepted, this will result in broader discussion by traditional media. Consider approaching university newspapers that may report on key local issues. Frequently, student reporters are committed to presenting "both sides" of an issue.

- **Radio.** Look for radio opportunities. Talk radio and news radio are almost always hungry for good discussion topics and factual analysis. A good story will be picked up. Once you have your list of radio contacts, look within your association and your other coalition partners for ways to affect the members of the media you need to reach. Look for ways to include them in your own coalition and develop surrogate spokespeople for your issue. Be sure to frame the issues broadly enough that you can maintain an ongoing relationship with your coalition.

The media as a whole seem to prefer a single spokesperson. It better fulfills their deadline requirements if there is someone they can consistently call for comment on a given issue. On the other hand, this can be a sure-fire way to generate group rivalries. Also be aware that reporters tend to move to different jobs; be prepared to build new working relationships again every year or so.

The publisher of the daily newspaper generally is active in community affairs and the Chamber of Commerce. Look for ways to bring decision-makers for the paper into your regular coalition building efforts. Look to use the administrative procedures of the paper or television station to discuss editorial policy or bias.

Conclusions

It is becoming more and more difficult for an association to affect major governmental issues, particularly in the face of a well-organized or well-financed opponent. Coalitions are becoming necessary, not just to lend legitimacy to the message, but as the only way to marshal sufficient resources to consistently win over the hearts and minds of your elected officials, your neighborhood leadership, and the predisposition of the entire community.

- Coalitions are the tools that allow you to expand your effectiveness well beyond your own resources. A coalition can increase your individual power two-, five-, or tenfold.

- Realize that much of a coalition is simple networking. It involves gathering information, organizing for a task, and then carrying out your plan.

- Assess the importance of your issues. Special-purpose coalitions that exist for short duration depend on the legitimacy of the common goal. Frankly, if the issue is important enough, some of the group can be "carried" as a name-only ally. There is no shame in being carried if another coalition member has greater resources or clout with a particular issue. It is naïve not to recognize the need for allies and multiple faces for the financially strong.

- Make sure there is mutual interest. If you have a permanent group that meets monthly, those meetings will not last if there is not a common goal or benefit, even if the benefit is social or networking.

- Delegate. Don't try to do everything yourself. The membership in the association and their staff must be active in groups (many consider community involvement a key part of the sales end of their business).

The American Energy Alliance

Michael Smith, CAE

Formal coalitions have a stated goal, structure, and a decision-making body to meet their agendas. Ad hoc coalitions come together on a single issue and then disperse. Their members may transcend party or economic lines and be competitors in other realms of endeavor.

One coalition that worked well for the National Association of Manufacturers (NAM) was the American Energy Alliance (AEA) coalition. NAM recruited more than 2,500 coalition members, activated them, and put structures into place in less than forty days.

Activate Your Coalition

The following are the major activities undertaken by the AEA coalition:

- assembled a diverse group to attack the Clinton British thermal unit (BTU) tax based on energy consumption; AEA said the fees would cost American businesses $10 billion in taxes based on the use of energy as a raw material;

- involved farmers and consumers who are not traditionally in coalition groups and used the public message that American families, senior citizens, and many others would be hurt by a tax based on BTU consumption;

- emphasized that unfair taxation issues were important to fight; once the precedent is set to unfairly tax certain business sectors, more arguments could be made to tax business in other ways; and

- retained Burson-Marstellar consultants for state work, to fight the issue in capitals of states with high energy use.

The Challenge

The major challenge for AEA was to position the BTU tax as an "every man's" issue. AEA received $2 million in funding from its members and from allies in energy-related lobbying groups. It used public opinion to convince senators and members of the House of Representatives that this was a bad bill. In the process, AEA saved the business community $10 billion.

The role of the chief elected officer (CEO) or chair in a coalition is key. NAM president Jerry Jasinowski agreed to be AEA's chair. The CEO is not the government relations expert, and roles of all coalition members must be clearly delineated to ensure success. NAM had to make sure its coalition partners and all 2,500 of its newly acquired members felt AEA was waging this fight on their behalf.

Each coalition member had to be empowered to act for the unit— not just to meet its own independent goals. Thus, even though energy producers and farmers disagreed on a compromise to the energy issue, all views expressed were in opposition to the BTU tax and no alternative forms of taxation were suggested to replace this revenue (including the gasoline tax, which was ultimately adopted).

Methods of Communication

The role of committees within AEA was even stronger. Committee members were asked to broker information to their own members. The newsletter, grassroots, policy, coalition, and building teams were given free reign to move forward quickly. The committees may not have always been synergistic, but they were always responsive to the coalition members.

AEA used a high level of communication technology (broadcast fax, telephone calls, and follow-up) to build excitement. Also, a major press conference was held at the National Press Club in Washington, D.C., to kick off the coalition group. It included opposition from every major business group in Washington. Led by Jasinowski, the AEA press conference made national headlines as it directly attacked the Clinton administration's budget program and key revenue ideas. AEA stood firm on the position that the BTU tax should not be permitted to move forward, and it—as a coalition of business lobbying groups—would not negotiate on this item.

Measurements of Success

"A coalition will sell itself if you are right on the issue," says Eben Tisdale, general manager of public affairs with Hewlett Packard. "People whom you did not even think of will come over in the transom."

Attracting support from unlikely sources is a sign of your success. Try to show broad-based appeal by inviting more than the predictable industry groups to join your coalition. In the case of AEA, getting the farmers and the farm bureaus on board was a key element.

In the end, the Clinton administration backed off on the tax. The nail was put in the coffin when Senators Breaux (D-La.) and Boren (D-Okla.), both from high energy-producing states, agreed to vote against the president in the Senate budget version of the bill.

Beginning Your Coalition

The American Society of Association Executives can be a helpful resource in the coalition process. Its Government Relations Section Council and Government Affairs Committee have a coalition-building and networking directory that can help bring about the effective coalition support you need. The golden rule of coalition building is to never let the decision-making process bog you down so much that the team doesn't have the freedom to act.

Coalition leaders have to invigorate the participants before they will want to participate. Bringing people together on a common problem can be exciting, and you need to reward the individual contributions of your coalition members.

Shaping Public Policy

The following are tips for building a coalition:

1. The two-party system is less influential, and third-party organizations will continue to gain strength as "voices of the people."

2. You can influence policy by creating a strong response during the development phases. Because traditional power centers in Washington are waning, junior representatives may have a chance to serve on a powerful committee or become a swing vote for business.

3. The media also play a large role in shaping the public and legislative agenda; you should use your coalition to position an issue effectively in the media.

The PARCA Coalition

Richard Miller

The experiences of the PARCA coalition—known formally as the Patient Access to Responsible Care Alliance—demonstrate the development and growth, over a substantial period of time, of an active coalition effort that is supported by several professional and trade associations that share common legislative goals at the federal level.

The primary goal of PARCA is to advance legislation that will establish, for the first time at the federal level, a comprehensive set of "patient and provider protections" that would apply to managed care and other health insurance plans. These protections are currently exempt from similar legislative or regulatory efforts at the state level, by virtue of a federal legislative preemption known as the Employee Retiree Income Security Act (ERISA).

Origins of the Coalition

The PARCA coalition and its efforts are supported by a broad and diverse group of organizations concerned about health policy issues— most notably, the effect the rapid growth of managed care is having on the quality and delivery of health care in America. Presently at the core of the coalition—helping to guide its policies and steer its day-to-day operations—are a dozen, well-established health professional associations, most of which represent the interests of non-medical-doctor (MD) health providers, such as nurse anesthetists, doctors of chiropractic, dentists, nurse midwives, psychologists, and so forth.

Most of the organizations that make up the core of the coalition have a track record of working together, from time to time, on matters of common interest at the federal level; some cooperative efforts date back several years. All of them were actively engaged in the debate over national health care reform, and the immediate origins of the PARCA coalition can be traced back to the collapse of the national health reform debate in late 1994.

Effort Launched from the Ashes of National Health Reform

In the fall of 1994, after a prolonged public debate, the Clinton-led effort to pass universal health care reform collapsed. Pressure to solve America's health care "crisis" evaporated under blistering attacks and adverse publicity. In a little over two years, a fickle and jittery American public went from demanding health care reform to breathing a collective sigh of relief that the specter of federal-led, Clintonesque reform had been avoided. The ill-fated effort proved a disaster for the Clinton administration, paving the way for a Republican take-over of Congress.

For the American Chiropractic Association (ACA), a leader in the PARCA coalition, the collapse of the national health care reform debate was a mixed blessing. True, an imperfect health reform scheme was avoided. But while the public and political focus was on Washington, the managed care industry continued to take over ever-larger segments of the unregulated health care marketplace and, in the process, served to cut off, in rapidly growing numbers, patient access to chiropractic care. Similar patient access and choice-of-provider problems were also faced by other provider groups that now make up the PARCA coalition. All of these provider groups are increasingly threatened and economically disadvantaged by the rapid growth of ERISA-governed managed care health insurance care plans, which often restrict non-MD provider participation, reimbursement, and autonomy in their plans, and routinely engage in what these provider organizations would characterize as discriminatory practices against their members. These provider organizations also assert that these and similar activities prevalent in managed care plans are not only harmful to their individual membership but are also harmful to the best interests of millions of their patients, whose interests and concerns they claim to represent as well.

Seeking to prepare itself for the next iteration of health reform and seeking to address its managed care concerns, ACA hosted a meeting with representatives of consumer and non-MD health provider groups in late 1994 in Washington, D.C. There, ACA outlined a strategy to build a coalition of organizations to push legislation that would address managed care concerns in the 104th Congress. Although the American Medical Association (AMA) had unveiled a Patient Protection Act during the recent health reform battle, ACA officials noted that most of the patient and provider protections included in the comprehensive health reform bills as they advanced through committee were due to aggressive lobbying by non-MD groups and medical specialty societies operating largely independently and sometimes in outright competition with the AMA. Although the future of health reform would be quite uncertain under a new Republican-controlled Congress, ACA argued that the non-MD provider community had no choice but to ensure that its views were prominent in any future health reform debate. Additionally, managed care abuses would have to be brought under control, and patient access issues would have to be dealt with. ACA argued that the most effective way to deal with these issues was to develop a coalition-based comprehensive patient-provider legislative package and to unveil it as quickly as possible in the new 104th Congress. This would ensure that the non-MD version would be the "first on the block" and would ideally achieve a level of prominence ahead of any other health reform proposal that might be unveiled.

A Legislative Package to Unify and Bind the Coalition Is Developed

A general consensus to proceed was reached at that first concept meeting held in the fall of 1994. The coalition began its work in a very informal and loosely structured manner, with the ACA representative serving, by consensus, as the coalition's chair. As a follow-up, ACA hosted a series of coalition meetings throughout the remainder of 1994 and in the winter of 1995 to develop a legislative proposal. Eventually, to facilitate the drafting of the coalition proposal, the services of a well-known firm of Washington health policy experts was retained. The coalition also retained as a consultant for the project a former legislative counsel to Sen. Paul Wellstone (D-Minn.). Wellstone had been the only member of the Senate to introduce a version of AMA's Patient Protection Act during the debate over the Clinton plan, and the consultant had handled the staff work on that bill. Funds to retain these consultants were provided by ACA. However, other groups in the coalition provided staff manpower and expertise to help fine tune the proposal and to ensure that it would be acceptable to their constituencies. Despite ACA's initial exclusive funding of the coalition, the coalition operated in a democratic manner, with all groups having an equal voice in the formation of the legislative package and in developing strategy to advance the proposal.

The Coalition Adopts a Formal Name and Seeks Introduction of Their Proposal

After several months of drafting and revising, the coalition finalized a draft legislative proposal in the spring of 1995 and began the process of seeking original sponsors to introduce the bill in Congress. Concurrent with finalizing the draft bill, the loosely structured coalition agreed to call itself the Coalition for Health Care Choice and Accountability (CHCCA), with ACA's representative continuing to serve as the coalition's chair.

Sponsors Recruited

Members of CHCCA fanned out to recruit proposal sponsors—one Democrat and one Republican. ACA played an instrumental role in recruiting then-Congressman Bill Brewster (D-Okla.) to be the chief democrat sponsor. Brewster had worked closely with ACA and another coalition member, the National Community Pharmacists Association, on any-willing-provider and point-of-service issues during the Clinton health reform battle. The American Dental Association, another active member of CHCCA-recruited newly elected Representative Charlie Norwood (R-Ga.), formerly a practicing dentist, to be the chief Republican sponsor. On Sept. 27, 1995, the coalition's bill was introduced as H.R. 2400, the Family Health Care Fairness Act of 1995, and CHCCA grew to over sixty member organizations formally supporting the coalition effort and H.R. 2400. Continuing as the exclusive funding source for the coalition's major activities, ACA paid for the development and printing of various coalition promotional materials and for the establishment of a coalition office with telephone and fax headquartered in the offices of a Washington, D.C., lobbying firm.

Slow Going in the 104th Congress

ACA continued to chair and fund the coalition during the two years of the 104th Congress. Health issues in Congress during this period, however, were dominated by debate over the Kassebaum-Kennedy "health portability act" and Republican attempts to reform the federal Medicare program. Under these circumstances, promoting H.R. 2400 was difficult. CHCCA had to be content with keeping the issue of regulating managed care alive, while trying to build support for future action. Efforts to find a suitable Senate sponsor in the 104th Congress were not successful, but in the House, a bipartisan group of 41 members ultimately cosponsored H.R. 2400. Although one set of managed care hearings was held in the House Commerce Committee and the coalition had laid important groundwork, the 104th Congress adjourned without taking action on H.R. 2400 or any significant managed care legislation. For many in the coalition, this was a period of some demoralization, marked by an apparent lack of major progress. Many participants in the coalition considered abandoning the effort. However, the prestigious American Public Health Association's endorsement for adoption of federal legislation based on H.R. 2400's principles was a notable achievement in 1996.

The Groundwork Is Laid for the 105th Congress

CHCCA continued to strategize over how to move H.R. 2400 and the coalition's concerns forward in the 105th Congress. By this time, key ally Bill Brewster had retired from Congress. Charles Norwood became the key Congressional champion of the cause—and demonstrated a personal level of commitment that helped reinvigorate the coalition. H.R. 2400 would have to be reintroduced because a new Congress was to convene in January 1997.

The Proposal Is Modified and the Coalition Adopts a New Name

In strategy sessions with Representative Norwood, modifications were made to H.R. 2400 to broaden its appeal. The new bill was renamed the Patient Access to Responsible Care Act (PARCA). To emphasize its support for this version of H.R. 2400, the coalition changed its name to the Patient Access to Responsible Care Alliance. The PARCA bill, now numbered as H.R. 1415, was introduced by Representative Norwood in the House and by Sen. Alphonse D'Amato (R-N.Y.) in the Senate on April 23, 1997. In the House, the PARCA bill was introduced with 65 cosponsors. By early 1997, other coalition members, in addition to ACA, agreed to make regular contributions and share the cost of the coalition. This pooling of resources allowed the PARCA coalition to retain a professional lobbying firm to help promote the bill and later allowed the coalition to retain the services of a professional public relations firm to help build media support for PARCA. With the active lobbying of PARCA coalition members, the number of cosponsors had grown in the House to 117 by mid-summer.

Hearings Showcase the PARCA Bill and Highlight Managed Care Problems

By the time hearings were held in the fall of 1997 before the House Commerce Committee and House Education and Workforce Committee, the cosponsor list had grown to 186. These hearings helped highlight the problems faced by consumers in managed care plans and provided Representative Norwood, who testified at both hearings, with an opportunity to showcase the PARCA bill and gain media attention for it.

The Opposition Prepares to Strike Back

The popularity of the Norwood PARCA bill and the public's continuing dissatisfaction with managed care abuses resonated on Capitol Hill during the first session of the 105th Congress. The coalition's stunning progress in rapidly building up the cosponsor list for PARCA caught the bill's opponents—the managed care industry, the insurance industry, and major employer groups—off guard. Despite a continuing series of horror stories in the media during 1997, it wasn't until summer that the managed care industry began to take the PARCA bill seriously. When hearings were held in the fall of 1997, the industry was clearly in political trouble. A public opinion poll released on Oct. 22, 1997, paid for by the PARCA coalition and conducted by the Wirthlin Group, reported that there was strong consumer support for choice of health care professionals, that managed care organizations should not be able to deny treatment, and that health maintenance organizations (HMOs) should be legally accountable when inappropriate decisions result in patient harm. Managed care, which previously resisted all efforts to impose federal standards, also showed major signs of division when three large nonprofit HMOs publicly called for the passage of "enforceable federal standards" in the early fall. The majority of the managed care industry, joined by employer organizations, remains adamantly opposed to the PARCA bill and has announced the allocation of a million dollars for the first phase of a campaign to defeat the bill. Additionally, elements of the industry, including the Health Insurance Association of America

(HIAA), have enlisted the support of key members of the House and Senate Republican leadership to fight the bill's passage. Shortly before adjournment of the first session of the 105th Congress, House Majority Leader Dick Armey branded the PARCA effort as "Clinton Care II" and urged its defeat.

A Battle Looms in 1998

Despite mounting industry opposition, by the time the first session of the 105th Congress adjourned, the cosponsor list in the House had grown to over 200 members. 1998 is an election year, and the battle lines are clearly drawn. With continuing media attention focused on problems of managed care, some observers predict Congress will pass some form of managed care legislation in 1998. The opposition to PARCA, though playing catch-up in the House, has formidable support in the Senate, where PARCA has yet to make major inroads. The opposition also has financial resources that far outstrip those of the PARCA coalition and ACA. Only time will tell if the efforts of the PARCA coalition will swing the tide enough to pass some form of the PARCA bill in 1998.

Effective Coalition Work the Key to Success Thus Far

The final battle over the PARCA bill has not yet played itself out. What is clear, however, is that, through effective coalition work, the proponents of the PARCA bill have, over a period of three years, advanced their proposal from the concept stage to where it is now regarded as the preeminent managed care standards bill in Congress. Thus, the issues and principles contained in the bill are virtually guaranteed to be included in any serious debate over the future of managed care legislation—and the organizations making up the core of the coalition are likely to find themselves "at the table." There are several reasons for this:

- The PARCA coalition, like many coalitions, needed a driving force to launch and maintain the effort, particularly during its formative period. ACA played this critical role.

- The concept for forming the coalition and developing a coalition-acceptable legislative package was a fundamentally sound proposal, with broad potential appeal to the diverse elements of the coalition.

- Although initial funding was supplied exclusively by ACA, great pains were taken to ensure that the development of the coalition's legislative proposal and strategy was "democratic," with significant efforts on ACA's behalf to ensure that participants in the coalition effort remained empowered and, thus, committed to the coalition's agenda.

- Staff representatives from a variety of coalition-supporting organizations provided significant manpower and creative input into the development of the agreed-to legislative package. This was a task that, in and of itself, required several months of effort.

- The coalition partners shared and continue to share the lobbying and grassroots workload effectively, with all groups participating in coordinated coalition activities and having a say in what those activities should be.

- When disagreements over policy and/or strategy occurred, they were settled amicably, with groups agreeing to compromise their views or position for the greater good of the coalition.

- As momentum and enthusiasm developed, a core group of coalition organizations demonstrated and continues to demonstrate its commitment to the effort, via monthly financial commitments to coalition projects, including lobbying and public relations activities.

- When it became necessary to modify elements of the original proposal (H.R. 2400) to have it successfully introduced as the PARCA bill in the 105th Congress, the coalition was able to adopt a realistic view and work through that process in a timely and efficient manner.

- The coalition remains open-minded to working with other groups to expand the reach and influence of coalition effort.

- The government relations representatives of the various groups making up the coalition have worked hard and in a very professional manner, with high regard for the needs and concerns of their colleagues and the constituencies they represent.

NOTE

The following ASAE members contributed to this chapter:
- *Dennis Brown, CAE, Equipment Leasing Association*
- *Aubrey King, CAE, Travel and Tourism Government Affairs Council*
- *Colleen Nolan, American Association of Oral and Maxillofacial Surgeons*
- *Harry Savio, Texas Capitol Area Builders Association*
- *Michael Smith, CAE, National Association of Manufacturers' Manufacturing Institute*
- *Richard Miller, Miller and Company*

Preparing and Delivering Effective Testimony

William A. Franco

THE CORE MISSION of most trade associations or professional societies is government relations. The ability to provide association members with timely analyses of trends on key legislative and regulatory issues and strategic and technical guidance for their policy and advocacy efforts is critical to any government relations program.

Most government relations departments serve as information resource and clearinghouse centers to assist members in the development of unified industry positions. When necessary, associations participate in coalitions to lobby in support of or in opposition to legislation and regulation that directly or indirectly affects their related industries.

But perhaps one of the greatest challenges that association government relations staff face is effectively testifying before legislative committees or regulatory bodies. Even though this can be a daunting task, the opportunity to testify usually allows you to advocate your position in a very public manner and educate members of the committee, as well as other interested parties, on your key issues.

There are some straightforward steps that associations should take to prepare effective testimony. First, given that there can be literally hundreds of pieces of legislation or proposed regulations facing any one industry at the federal or state level, engaging association members and committees early on in the planning phase to prioritize key issues is critical to the success of a government relations program. Second, careful pre-legislative and regulatory planning requires that objectives for priority issues are clearly defined. Finally, appropriate allocation of resources and staffing should be given so that the association effectively represents its members' interests.

Prepare for the Hearing

Once you have taken the necessary steps to prioritize your legislative strategy, association staff and members (including their lobbyists) must work closely together in advance of hearings to agree on what areas the testimony will cover. Often, it can be difficult for association members to achieve total consensus. Therefore, association members will often give staff the necessary direction, flexibility, and latitude to carry out the organization's legislative objectives and priorities.

It is always critical for associations and members to be mindful of the numerous steps required in the legislative process for a bill to become law, including the governor's or president's veto pen. It is important to know how many committees of jurisdiction may be interested in a particular piece of legislation. If the legislation is favorable to your organization's interests, it is critical to identify who your natural lobbying allies might be. It is also helpful to know whether or not your association members are willing to take an active role in the process by writing their own letters concerning the legislation. Finally, it is helpful to have in place a mechanism to educate and inform your members on legislative strategies and developments as they unfold during the process.

As testimony is prepared, staff should carefully review materials that the association has developed on a particular issue—for example, news releases, written testimony, and policy statements. Seasoned legislative committee staff will do their homework on your association, members, and key issues to identify inconsistencies in your position.

Preparing effective testimony also requires knowing who your audience is. Your audience obviously includes members of the committee, their staffs, the media, and other interested parties—both supporters and opponent of your point of view. Your testimony is a good opportunity to stimulate your own members to work with you on a key issue for their association.

When preparing your testimony, pay attention to the special concerns of legislative members and staff. To be effective, you should play "devil's advocate" to carefully understand what will be the likely approach during hearings from both proponents and opponents of the legislation.

It is the function of a witness not only to communicate with his or her audience, but to attempt to persuade them as well. An effective witness finds common ground shared by legislators on which he or she can build an appealing argument. To that end, it may be beneficial to pick as your spokesperson someone who happens to live in the state or district of the chair or some other key member of the committee. The goal of your witness should be to deliver a substantive message while simultaneously leaving a positive impression with the committee.

Preparing Your Written and Oral Testimony

Witnesses should prepare statements in essentially two ways. First, the statement should be prepared in writing for the official hearing record. Many committees have their own special requirements for written testimony, including number of copies, size of paper, line spacing, and font size. It is also important to be sensitive to the committee's general guidelines on the length of written statements submitted for the official record.

Second, oral testimony should be prepared. Many witnesses prefer to read or paraphrase from a written text. If oral testimony is given this way, witnesses should highlight the written testimony, being as brief as possible. The committee will gain more from the testimony of a witness who allows for questions and answers and a focused discussion on the issue, rather than one who uses all of the allotted time in presenting testimony itself.

During oral testimony, it is important to summarize what is in the official record version, emphasizing only the key points. This should take no longer than five minutes, or whatever is allowed by the committee's chairman. In fact, most committees will have specific time limits of which you should be aware in advance. Your witness should practice his or her testimony with trade association staff and colleagues to be sure it tracks with the committee's general hearing guidelines.

A committee's members are often not experts on your specific policy or technical issue, so it is important to make testimony understandable. Don't assume that the committee will understand technical industry terms, abbreviations, or association policy. It is also important to adhere strictly to the rules of the committee chair. Attention to the chairman's rules helps to put the witness in the good graces of the committee.

It is very important that witnesses not answer a legislator's question unless they know the answer. Trying to guess the answer will immediately destroy their credibility as a witness and destroy whatever favorable impressions they may have made during their oral statement. It is better for witnesses to indicate that they will follow up with the committee or committee staff to provide a response to the question with written documentation.

When preparing both oral and written testimony, the statement should be reviewed by the appropriate members of the association prior to the hearing in order for them to make suggestions. Remember, written testimony is for the details, oral testimony is for discussion at the hearing.

Additional Prehearing Work

Before a hearing, association staff work should involve more than the preparation of written and oral testimony. Staff may prepare suggested questions for legislative members and their staff. This can help your witnesses get their point across and underscore critical elements of concern about the legislation. The right questions from legislators to your opponents also can help to bolster your arguments.

With respect to your association's written testimony, it is a general courtesy to deliver copies to all members of the committee. Prior to the hearing, it is also appropriate to distribute press releases to the media and copies of your testimony for general distribution. Finally, be sure you know where the hearing is being held. Be there on time. Legislative schedules are often subject to change, so be prepared to wait.

Post-hearing Work

What you do after the hearing is almost as important as your prehearing preparation. A number of basic tasks should be considered. Send follow-up thank you letters to the committee and staff for the opportunity to appear. If the committee did not vote favorably for your position, don't despair—you may still have another opportunity legislatively to improve the legislation through amendments or other means. The important point is to maintain your base of support and also continue to reach out to your opponents throughout the legislative process.

Request a stenographic copy of the witnesses' remarks. It is not uncommon for mistakes to be made, and it's always important that every effort be made to "protect the record." Generally, the substance of what was stated cannot be changed, but witnesses are permitted to correct improper grammar and phrasing. It is always important to follow up immediately with the committee staff to seek their feedback on the hearing and respond to any unresolved issues.

Finally, it can be helpful to reconvene your association members to discuss what occurred during the hearing and possible next steps. Keeping your members involved at every step of the legislative or regulatory process is critical to your success on any given issue.

Conclusion

There is no single formula for delivering effective testimony. A great deal depends on the complexity and nature of the issue, the capability and skill of your witness, the political environment of the committee, and the quality of the preparation that is expended beforehand by association staff in developing an overall strategy for delivering your message.

One key to successful testimony is to get your members involved early. Involving association members at each critical step of the process, particularly with regard to the substance of written and oral testimony, will help to ensure success. Attention to the basic fundamentals outlined above will help to advance your association members' key legislative and regulatory goals and objectives when testifying before legislative and regulatory bodies.

Creating Effective Legislative Newsletters

Aaron K. Trippler

GOVERNMENT AFFAIRS NEWSLETTERS should be a flexible, timely, and effective way to communicate with your members and other interested parties. Newsletters can convey information about activities to members, ask for ideas and suggestions for future projects, and spur discussion on topics of interest to the membership or profession.

Before embarking on publishing a government affairs newsletter, the government affairs professional or other individual responsible for the newsletter should look beyond layouts, headlines, jargon, and other strategies to creating a successful publication. It is important to know the reasons behind publishing the newsletter in the first place.

As an association government affairs professional, you are in the business of government affairs, not publishing. You are responsible for providing information on the impact or potential impact of government involvement in the lives of your members or profession/industry. At times, you must solicit advice on how to affect the outcome of government actions.

There are two rules of thumb to putting together an association newsletter. The first is to provide insight, not opinions. It is your job to report the facts, not to provide your opinion on what the government is doing. Of course, it is your job to provide insight into what you think the outcome of a specific government action will be; however, providing this insight is different from providing an opinion on the issue.

The second rule of thumb is to stay out of politics. Although this may sound like a contradiction because your job *is* politics, keep in mind that your job is to implement association policy, not to make policy. Unless your particular position requires you to involve yourself in politics, stay away from it. There is no need to mention the party designation of the many senators and representatives in your newsletter. Issues are issues—regardless of the party. Readers are quite capable of knowing which side of the aisle a particular elected official resides (i.e., state the sponsor as Rep. Jim Ramstad of Minnesota, not Rep. Jim Ramstad, Republican from Minnesota). Of course, there is nothing wrong with stating the obvious—that one party or the other is leading the charge of the opposition on a particular issue.

Writing your government affairs newsletter should be an exercise in staying on top of the issues. If you are asked to make a five-minute presentation before the board of directors on the association's government affairs issues, what would you say? An effective government affairs newsletter is the same as the "30-second sound bite," but in printed form.

Goals of a Government Affairs Newsletter

Creating an effective legislative newsletter may include the following goals:

1. Protect the membership. If protecting the membership is not in your government affairs mission statement, it should be.
2. Enhance the membership. Build up as much credibility for your members as possible.
3. Inform the membership. Communication is still the key to success. Your members need to be kept informed of the activities taking place and reminded that they are receiving a good value for their dues dollars.
4. Update interested parties. Your audience should include policy makers and other interested parties who want to know what your association is doing and saying. They will consider you an important resource.
5. Provide the membership with a sense of ownership. Members should feel that they are responsible for some of the success.
6. Influence the issues. When the word is spread, the views of your association do have an effect on the issues, however small.

7. Focus association direction. There are times when the membership needs to be guided a little more than usual. A newsletter can start or continue the process of member involvement.

8. Listen and learn. No matter how large or small the newsletter, feedback will be forthcoming. This is one way the government affairs professional has to learn what members are saying. Invite feedback.

The Informal Rules

Know Your Subject

You should understand the information you are attempting to convey to the reader. Keep the issues important to the association and its membership in clear focus. Take the time to learn about the profession of its membership. You'll be able to make intelligent decisions when you understand their needs and concerns.

Know Your Audience

You should be trying to make contact with "movers and shakers." It is not necessary to write the newsletter for the entire membership; save this type of article for a monthly publication that reaches the entire membership. If additional parties are privy to the newsletter—consider it a bonus.

Read Everything

You should read newspapers, periodicals, trade publications, and other newsletters to keep up-to-date on the issues of importance to your association and its membership. This consumes a lot of time, but it is worth it. You need to know who is saying what, what your allies and competitors are saying, and what they are doing.

Keep It Simple

Write for readability. Design for a quick turnaround. The newsletter should be no more than four pages long. Look to your own experiences; one-page articles that appear in your in-box are usually read immediately. Those three- and four-page articles usually are put aside for later.

Organization

Select a format and stick to it. For example, you may choose to organize your newsletter in the order of federal legislation, state legislation, regulatory activity, and other issues. Readers like to feel comfortable with a publication, regardless of its size. By organizing your newsletter in the same way each time, readers will know exactly what to look for and where it can be found.

Timeliness

Be flexible. Don't get hung up on putting out a newsletter on a specific timetable. No one knows for sure when government affairs activity will increase or decrease. Wait for the opportune time. The key is to have something to say. Perhaps it is enough to publish the newsletter eight or nine times a year. Allow yourself the flexibility to determine when the next issue is needed, not when it is expected. Readers who consistently receive a newsletter on the first of the month with little timely news in it will eventually skip reading it all together. If you are flexible and publish the newsletter when you actually have something to say, readers will tend to read it immediately because they know the information is timely and applicable to them.

Distribution

How you distribute your newsletter depends on your financial resources and the preferences of readers. Should you send your newsletter via broadcast fax? Should it be mailed? Is e-mail the answer? Perhaps a combination of all should be used. Different readers have different preferences. Experiment a little and ask for suggestions.

Also, be sure to compile a list of additional interested parties to receive every issue of the newsletter. These are the policy makers and others you are attempting to reach with all of your additional efforts. A newsletter is one of the simplest and cheapest tools for accomplishing this task. Remember, it's not only government affairs—it's public relations.

Special Alerts

Special alerts can be useful for late-breaking information or a "call to action." But use these alerts sparingly. Educate readers so they understand that a special alert is important and demands their immediate attention. If a reader receives more than three or four special alerts in the course of a year, you have lost the sense of urgency an alert should impart.

It Pays the Mortgage

Putting out an effective government affairs newsletter is part of the job. If you expect to move up the career ladder, show some initiative. If the information you have is important to you, it may be important to others. Successful government affairs executives know what is important and what is not.

The Formal Rules

The following outline can serve as a more formal guide to producing an effective government affairs newsletter:

I. **Purpose of a Government Affairs Newsletter**

    A. Why have a legislative newsletter? Define your goals.
- To educate members so they can take action.
- To get the message out.
- To communicate with professionals outside of your organization.
- To call for action in opposition to or support of a proposed measure.
- To form a coalition of interests by drawing together parties with similar interests.
- To get a message to legislators.
- To gain recognition for association initiatives.
- To follow up on information earlier circulated—keep member up-to-speed on legislative activity.

    B. Who are your audiences? Target your audiences and tailor your newsletter to influence those you truly wish to affect. Identify your primary audience and tailor the newsletter to it, while keeping your secondary audience(s) in mind.
- Members
- Prospective members
- Other interested parties
- Legislators
- The media
- Potential clients

    C. How often will you publish?
- Weekly
- Monthly
- During legislative sessions

D. Budget
  - Staff
  - Printing
  - Mailing—can it be distributed with other association publications?

II. What Goes in It: Newsletter Content
A. Basic news writing guidelines
  - Use short sentences.
  - Use active rather than passive voice.
  - Don't use jargon.
  - Explain what your organization is doing about an issue.
  - Identify your sources.
  - Use quotes.

B. Basic Newswriting: The Pyramid Style of Writing. When writing articles you should put the most important information at the beginning and work your way down. Then, if the article is too long, cut from the bottom.
Writing a lead.
  - A lead is a one-sentence paragraph. It's a summary statement.
  - The lead hooks readers—makes them want to read more.
  - It answers the questions who, what, when, where, why, and how.
  - The lead should feature the single most important piece of information.

C. Make legislation understandable. Your job is to:
  - Transform legislation/laws into reader-friendly informational articles.
  - Highlight the important information in a proposed piece of legislation or new law.
    a. How will it affect your members' business/industry/profession?
    b. What is the local/state/national impact?
    c. Give practical examples of what the legislation/law would do.
    d. What is the political background of the proposal/law—who is behind it?
  - Take your summary and turn it into a readable and interesting article that will make your audience want to stay tuned.

- Is there any member action that may be necessary or useful to help/defeat the proposed legislation? What can members do to actively participate in debate of the issue?

D. Write inspiring copy—informing readers and spurring them to act.
- You're not going to spur anyone to action if you put them to sleep—make your articles interesting and relevant to your readers.
- If you're constantly screaming "fire," your readers aren't going to pay attention to you after a while.
- Avoid the two most overused words in writing about legislation: "onerous" and "devastating."
- Show me, don't tell me.

III. Appearance is Almost Everything
A. Image
- Whether you're aware of it or not, a newsletter projects an image of your organization and your legislative program.
- Produce a sharp newsletter and enhance the image of your organization.
- Look at your newsletter as if you were an outsider—what does it say about your organization?

B. Develop an identity
- Use a consistent format.
- Adopt a logo.

C. Tips on readability
- Black type on white paper provides the best contrast.
- 10-point type is ideal.
- Approximately 58 characters across a column is comfortable for the eye.
- Bold and italic type faces call attention to words or phrases, but are hard to read in large blocks of copy.
- Screens draw the eye, but if they're too dark, the copy can be tough to read.
- White space is good.

(portions adapted from American Subcontractors Association, Inc.)

Political Action Committees and Campaign Involvement

Charlotte Herbert

IN A CLASSIC STATEMENT about the imperfections of democracy, Winston Churchill once said, "It has been said that Democracy is the worst form of government except all those other forms that have been tried from time to time." And few aspects of our American system of democracy are as ambiguous as campaign finance. Polls suggest many Americans regret that candidates for public office often need to devote half of their professional career to raising money. For many incumbent members of Congress, raising money is the least favorite part of their jobs. Prominent former senators Bill Bradley and Alan Simpson have said that they retired to avoid another grueling campaign and the fund-raising that goes along with it.

Most likely, your association membership has mixed feelings about campaign finance. However, it's the way the system works, and your association needs to be involved with the political process to have an impact on the issues before Congress that affect its membership. Trade associations, corporations, and labor unions spent a record amount of money in the last election cycle through political action committees (PACs) and political education funds. The Federal Election Commission (FEC) reports that PAC contributions in the 1995–96 election cycle to all federal candidates totaled $201 million, up 12 percent from the 1993–94 election cycle. Americans will likely contribute even more money to political campaigns in the future.

What Is the Purpose of Political Spending?

Today's political system requires a large influx of money from concerned citizens. The expenses and advertising involved with one full-time congressional campaign can be more than $500,000, and although a few wealthy candidates can fund most of their campaigns themselves, most candidates for Congress need to constantly raise money.

When several candidates win election to Congress with less than 1000 votes, an association's failure to invest in political races can mean a difference in control of a chamber. The last two congressional elections have included several very close races. Even more subtle, a failure to invest in certain candidates can mean more narrow majorities in committees or the absence of an important leader on an issue.

Charlotte Herbert

How Can an Association Implement Campaign Financing?

An incorporated trade association may not use its treasury funds for contributions or expenditures in connection with federal elections. To offset the financial clout of its opponents, an association often creates its own PAC and its own political education fund.

A PAC is the political voice of its association, and through it, association members can support candidates who support their agenda. An association establishes a PAC fund (known legally as a separate, segregated fund) so that it can make contributions to or expenditures on behalf of federal candidates and other committees. Money contributed to a PAC is held in a bank account separate from the general treasury.

A political education fund allows association members to educate the public on political issues. This fund comes from the association's general revenue and is thus subject to different restrictions than are PAC funds. Although an association cannot use this fund to endorse or oppose candidates for public office, it can use the fund to alert the public to issues of concern to the association. A political education fund is similar to "soft money" that political parties use for volunteer, grassroots party-building activities and, most important, for issue advocacy spending. In fact, under current law, money from political education funds can be donated to party committees as "soft money." The association should be certain to check with legal counsel before making any such contributions because major campaign reform proposals are being debated that could greatly restrict, or even ban, the giving and use of soft money or issue advocacy efforts.

When association members give to their association PAC or political education fund, they are speaking as part of a powerful collective of Americans in their particular industry or profession. The money goes further than it would if given as an individual contribution to a candidate. Congressional supporters of the association agenda know that association members are serious about their commitment when they combine their money into a PAC or political education fund.

How Does an Association Establish a PAC?

An organization must register a federal PAC with the FEC, the independent agency that enforces federal election law. A PAC must designate a treasurer, who is responsible for fulfilling the legal duties of the PAC and is personally liable if the duties are not fulfilled. Some PACs have a board of trustees who make decisions on PAC policy and disbursements. Having association members on the board of trustees confirms to the membership that the association PAC is run by the members, not by association employees.

How Does an Association Legally Operate a PAC?

The following is an outline of important rules concerning PACs for trade associations. Keep in mind that this list is not exhaustive and that somewhat different rules apply to the PACs of corporations and labor unions.

Who Can Give to an Association PAC?

The "restricted class" that an association PAC can solicit once permission for solicitation is granted consists of executive and administrative personnel of incorporated member companies who are paid on a salary rather than hourly basis and have policy-making, managerial, professional, or supervisory responsibilities. Among the individuals in the restricted class are officers; executives; and plant, division, and section managers.

Salaried foremen and other salaried lower-level supervisors who have direct supervision over hourly employees are not part of the restricted class. An association PAC cannot ask these or other basic employees for a PAC contribution.

Partnerships can give to the PAC unless they are incorporated. If only some partners are incorporated within a partnership, the partners who are incorporated cannot give. The other partners can give, but they must include a letter identifying which partners gave how much money.

Individuals who are not members of the association can give to its PAC only if no representatives of the association have solicited the individual. The PAC can only ask its members for contributions, according to the solicitation authorization rules.

Solicitation Authorization

The FEC prohibits any association member or other collection agent from asking another member to give to the association PAC unless the member has filled out and signed a solicitation approval form granting permission to be solicited. According to the FEC, the "principal contact" of a company must grant permission before a PAC can ask him or her or his or her executive and administrative personnel for a PAC contribution. The principal contact of a company is the person who has the most contact with the association.

The association PAC keeps a prior approval form on record to prove that the principal contact gave the association permission to ask for a PAC contribution from the principal contact or his or her restricted type of employees. An association can publish permission forms in its newsletters.

The principal contact for a company can grant approval for his or her executive and administrative employees to be solicited by checking off the appropriate box on the prior approval form for each year. If a principal contact does not want his or her employees to be solicited, the contact should check off the appropriate box. PACs should encourage approval to solicit member companies' restricted type of employees. An association may obtain prior approval from its members at the time dues are paid.

Technical Rules

Legally, if the spouse of an association member signs a PAC contribution check, the PAC has to credit the donation to the spouse unless the association member encloses a letter with the check explaining that the contribution is his or her contribution. The spouse and the member must both sign the letter. The FEC allows an association to solicit a spouse when the member signs a solicitation approval form, so an association member does not need the spouse to sign a solicitation authorization form.

A state PAC that is raising money for state and local candidates only has to follow state laws. If a state allows corporate contributions, a state PAC can take corporate checks.

Collecting PAC Money

The following are some basic rules to follow when collecting PAC money:

- An individual can give up to $5,000 per year to the PAC.

- The PAC can accept cash contributions of only $100 or less.

- A company PAC that is registered with the FEC can give up to $5,000 per year to the association PAC.

- Association members cannot use a payroll deduction or check-off plan to give money to the association PAC.

- An association state PAC may not make a contribution to the association federal PAC.

- In-kind contributions are gifts of goods, services, or property offered rather than a monetary contribution. In-kind contributions count against the contribution limits for candidates.

- A disclaimer similar to the one that follows is required in all solicitation forms. Not all associations use this particular language, and all associations should check with legal counsel to ensure that it uses the required language.

- "Contributions to _____ PAC are not tax deductible. Federal law requires political committees to report the name, mailing address, occupation, and name of employer of each individual who contributes in excess of $200 in a calendar year. The proposed contribution amounts are merely suggestions; you may choose to give more or less, or not at all. Contributions to _____ PAC are purely voluntary. _____ will not favor or disadvantage you by reason of the amount of your contribution or your decision not to contribute. You may refuse to contribute without reprisal. Corporate contributions or contributions by foreign nationals are prohibited. Paid for by _____ PAC."

Hosting Fund-raisers

Although direct mail may be an easy way to raise money, a personal solicitation from a fellow member is generally much more effective in raising more money from more members. Fund-raiser gatherings often are the most lucrative way to raise money for an association PAC.

Before hosting a PAC fund-raiser, an association should determine the most effective way to raise the largest amount of money. In an area where there are only a few members, a small dinner party at a high admission price might be the most effective way to raise money. In an area where members are numerous, but not financially able to donate large amounts, a cocktail party at a lower admission price might be more effective. In many cases, a combination of these two would allow an association to raise the maximum amount of money in a region.

The following are some examples of creative fund-raisers that have been proven successful:

- **Skeet Shoot.** An admission fee is charged, and prizes can be awarded for the top score. Shooting lessons beforehand are a possible addition.

- **PAC Auction.** Items are donated by or purchased from local members and businesses and are auctioned off to participants.

- **Boston Tea Party.** Held at the site of the original Boston Tea Party ship and museum and featuring a "Reinventing Government" theme. Can be tailored to historical attractions in other areas.

- **Miniature Golf Tournament.** A basic entrance fee is charged, with possible prizes for top score.

- **Blue Marlin Fishing Trip.** Participants pay a fixed price for the outing, which may include lunch beforehand or on the boat. The boat could be chartered, or money can be saved if a member owns a boat and is willing to donate its use. Prizes could be awarded for the biggest catches of the day.

- **Pig Roast.** The organization roasts a whole pig (or more or less, depending on number of attendees) and charges a flat fee to entrants, which covers all food and beverages (cash bar is also an option). Can be combined with other activities, such as country dancing or dance lessons.

- **Golf Getaway Promotion.** A golf tournament in which teams pay an entrance fee and compete for prizes.

- **Biking for Dollars.** Participants bicycle for a given distance, and find people to sponsor them by pledging a certain amount of money per mile ridden.

- **Sporting Events.** Attendance at sporting events works best when access to a special venue, such as a skybox, can be obtained. Admission is for a given price, and some sort of refreshments should be provided.

- **Casino Night.** A PAC can hold a casino night to raise PAC money depending on the gambling laws in the state where the event is held. In some states, casino night activities are not allowed. In other states, a PAC could hold a casino night provided that play money is used for gambling and that participants are not required to actually give money to the PAC. An association should check the state's gambling laws with its state PAC attorney.

An association can host a raffle to raise money for the association PAC, but the prize cannot be worth more than one-third of the money raised. If the prize is worth more, then the PAC has to pay the difference. If the prize is worth less than one-third of the money raised, then the association can pay for it using its own operating budget. In addition, any raffle contribution of $100 or more cannot be in cash form. Of course, all state and federal lottery laws have to be followed. If the raffle is interstate, the association must allow people to enter without paying if they so choose.

Support for Candidates

In addition to collecting money from the eligible association membership, PACs are responsible for distributing the money to friendly candidates. Here are some possible guidelines for making your association PAC's disbursement process consistent and principled:

- The association PAC should establish specific guidelines for awarding contributions.

- Association chapters, national staff, or the Washington, D.C. staff can initiate the process of contribution approval.

- The PAC trustees and the members in the region of the congressional candidate must approve the contribution.

- Positions on key issues and the total voting record of the candidate are taken into account.

- The association PAC has stringent standards for contributions to primaries or debt retirement.

- The association PAC contributes to only one candidate in an election race.

Political Education Fund

- A political education fund can be used only for political education purposes, such as the sponsorship of radio spots publicizing a bill moving through Congress.

- Political education funds can accept corporate money.

- There is no maximum contribution limit to the political education fund.

- Such funds may be tax deductible as a normal business expense.

- No forms are needed to contribute to the political education fund.

- The funds cannot be used to endorse a candidate or advocate the election or defeat of any candidates.

- Any company or individual can contribute to the political education fund regardless of position, even those who are not association members.

CHAPTER 12

Lobbying the Executive Branch

John Chwat

ASSOCIATION GOVERNMENT RELATIONS professionals should recognize that the executive branch of government—the White House, federal departments, and various agencies and commissions—can be key to implementing their legislative and regulatory strategies. Executive branch policies, rules, regulations, contacts, influence, and involvement can have a significant effect on the legislative process both before and after a bill becomes law. They also can affect how laws are interpreted, implemented, or diluted.

Rulemaking is the most important function undertaken by federal departments, agencies, and commissions. Rulemaking, or "regulation promulgation," defines the mission of every government agency and is critical in determining the direction of and issues involved in other bureaucratic functions, such as budgeting, funding programs, procurement and acquisition decision making, personnel management, and policy initiatives. Government relations professionals need to include this rulemaking process in their strategies.

The fundamental authority to issue rules is derived from statutes passed by Congress and signed by the president. The scope of these rules is limitless and is derived from a 1946 statute, the Administrative Procedure Act (APA). According to the APA, a "rule means the whole or part of an agency statement of general or particular applicability and future effect designed to implement, interpret, or prescribe law or policy."

Rules implement laws when statutes passed by Congress are substantive and provide sufficient direction on policies. Rules interpret laws when changing circumstances or events require agency intervention. Rules prescribe when Congress passes policies in statutes but does not provide enough details as to how to achieve these policies. APA permits the executive branch to fill any vacuum that has been left in a policy area or law by Congress, the president, or the courts.

Many successful government relations strategies are based on monitoring and seeking to affect executive branch rules. Proposed and final rules are drafted as agency documents and published in the *Federal Register,* which is published every federal working day. Rules appearing in the *Federal Register* are cited by volume and page number (for example, 56 FR 29187), beginning with volume 1 in 1936 and changing with each calendar year.

After regulations are published in the *Federal Register* as final rules, regulations are codified in the annual Code of Federal Regulations (CFR), which organizes rules in fifty distinct categories, referred to as titles and chapters, that correspond to public programs, policies, or agencies.

The primary function of the *Federal Register* and CFR system is to communicate to the public—including the business community, trade associations, and others—executive branch rulemaking activities. APA generally requires federal departments and agencies to publish a notice of proposed rulemaking in the *Federal Register* and to give interested persons the opportunity to submit written comments on the proposed rule.

Over the years, other laws have been passed to expand the scope of APA, including the Freedom of Information Act, the Government in the Sunshine Act, the Regulatory Flexibility Act, the Federal Advisory Committee Act, and the Negotiated Rulemaking Act. Citations for these and other relevant laws are listed at the end of this chapter.

Another source of rules and proposed rulemaking is the "Unified Agenda of Federal Regulatory and Deregulatory Actions," which is published in the *Federal Register* in October and April each year. The agenda, which usually fills three to five volumes, contains proposed rules that agencies have issued or expect to issue, current rules under agency review, final rules or actions the agency plans to take, and rules completed since the last agenda was published. For each rule, the agenda includes the name of a key contact person, with phone number, address, and agency listing. Also, each agenda item includes a brief review of the legal authority, CFR citation, subject matter of the rule, timetable for issuance, and other relevant information.

For government relations professionals, the agenda is a fundamental guidepost on rulemaking within the executive branch. All editions of the "Unified Agenda of Federal Regulatory and Deregulatory Actions" can be found on the World Wide Web (http://reginfo.gov/ua); these editions also can be searched on the Government Printing Office's Web site (http://www.access.gpo.gov). A more detailed discussion of rule-making procedures and regulatory issues can be found in three documents:

- *A Guide to Federal Agency Rulemaking,* by the Administrative Conference of the United States (Washington, D.C., 1991);

- *Rulemaking: How Government Agencies Write Law and Make Policy,* by Cornelius M. Kerwin (Congressional Quarterly Press, Washington, D.C., 1994); and

- "What It Is and How to Use It," in the *Federal Register* (Office of the Federal Register, Washington, D.C., 1992).

Results of a survey of over 180 Washington, D.C.-based interest groups participating in the regulatory process within the executive branch indicated that a variety of techniques are used to affect rules promulgated by the executive branch for interest groups, according to Kerwin in *Rulemaking: How Government Agencies Write Law and Make Policy.* The 180 organizations represented all sectors of the interest group community. The survey found that over 80 percent of all groups participated in the executive branch rulemaking process.

Although this survey confirms that there is widespread interest by industry groups in regulations directly affecting their member organizations, groups respond with different levels of intensity. For example, rules concerning beer labels, which are issued by the U.S. Department of the Treasury's Alcohol Tobacco and Firearms, affect brewers. These rules are monitored regularly by the Beer Institute and its member companies. Industry members meet with government regulators, and their comments, if appropriate, are submitted to the agency by the industry. Other examples are telephone companies' interest in Federal Communications Commission rules, cotton growers' interest U.S. Department of Agriculture regulations—the list is endless.

Most trade and industry groups maintain a regulatory affairs staff position or retain consultants experienced in advising on the regulatory agenda of the agencies involved in members' businesses. There are clear differences between lobbying the executive branch and lobbying the Congress.

Titles and Chapters in the Code of Federal Regulations

Government Officials and Federal Employees

Many government relations professionals may not be familiar with the "Plum Book," which is officially titled *U.S. Government Policy and Supporting Positions*. But presidential personnel offices and transition teams for presidential candidates and party officials and many others in Washington, D.C., are very familiar with this book. The Plum Book lists noncompetitive or political positions available for appointment by the White House within the executive branch.

The Plum Book can be helpful to government relations professionals who are researching the first segment in the federal government they should target for rulemaking issues, policy positions, and legislative impact on agency programs. These positions are highly political in that, when a new administration comes to the nation's Capitol, these are the positions that are filled with party-faithful, campaign supporters and the like.

For government relations professionals, this constituency is similar to key staff within Congress—the chief of staff to a member or a committee chief counsel—who serve as gatekeepers and who can influence elected officials and get things done. Department and agency political appointees are influenced by public opinion, congressional pressure, and party connections. Access at this level may be based on long-term relationships, White House or campaign networks, Capitol Hill connections, or other political connections. Access also can be based on the interest group (or industry) seeking to present its views on rules or policies.

The next constituency to address is civil servants, at various levels of professional development with the federal government. Many civil servants are highly specialized in their field—scientists, accountants, lawyers—or have spent many years studying and being involved in specific issues. Within vast bureaucracies, there are areas of specialization. One example is the cocoa bean expert in the tropical plants division of the U.S. Department of Agriculture who knows all about the bean's growing seasons, sales, imports, and exports. Information about the cocoa bean would be of key interest to chocolate manufacturers and other industry officials who are intimately involved in cocoa bean production, sales, and manufacturing.

This specialist in the Civil Service is similar to the congressional aid (legislative assistant or subcommittee staffer) who specializes in a particular subject area or set of bills by committee of jurisdiction. There, the similarity ends. Civil servants often are not easily approachable for lobbying purposes.

Ethics

Significant changes have been made to both the ethics and lobbying laws relating to federal government activities by lobbyists. These requirements are different from the rules governing ethics of House and Senate employees or members of Congress. For example, the Lobbying Disclosure Act of 1995 triggers a reporting requirement if government relations professionals—on behalf of their client or trade association—initiate any oral, written, or electronic communication with a covered executive branch or legislative branch official in the federal government. The communication described in the law includes:

- formulation, modification, or adoption of federal legislation;

- formulation, modification, or adoption of a federal rule, regulation, executive order, or any other program, policy, or position of the federal government;

- administration or execution of a federal program or policy (including the negotiation, award, or administration of a federal contract, grant, loan, permit, or license); and

- nomination or confirmation of a person for a position subject to Senate confirmation.

In addition to members of Congress, their staff, and committee employees, the law also covers many federal employees. Federal personnel covered by the disclosure law include the president; vice president; officers or employees of the executive office of the president; officials serving in an executive level I-V position, a "Schedule C" position or senior executive service position; and all employees who hold high-level ranks, such as secretaries, undersecretaries, assistant secretaries, general counsels, commissioners, inspectors general, and certain members of the uniformed services. The law also provides for many exceptions and details in its provisions, as well as information on the types of reports to file.

Equally significant to lobbying reporting requirements are regulations that involve receipt or prohibition of gifts by federal employees contained in rules from the Office of Government Ethics. These rules prohibit executive branch employees from accepting any gift or meal of $20 or more. Again, there are extensive requirements regarding what constitutes a gift as well as exceptions and other rules surrounding gift acceptance, honoraria, and various activities. Government relations professionals are likely to find *The Federal Lobbying Law Handbook* (edited by Jerald A. Jacobs, ASAE, Washington, D.C., 1993) (especially chapters 3 and 7, which relate to federal employees and government contractors) and *Compliance with Lobbying Laws and Gift Rules Guide* (edited by Barbara Timmer, Glasser Legal Works, N.J., 1996) to be useful resources.

Also, many federal departments and agencies maintain their own office of government ethics and require the filing of reports and other documents. The agencies and departments being targeted for government relations projects can be contacted directly.

General Accounting Office Reports

John Chwat

Congress may request investigations and reports from the General Accounting Office (GAO) on federal programs and expenditures. In general, GAO supports congressional oversight investigations of federal rulemaking, such as issues on delay in the issuance of rules, competence of an agency to manage or implement projects and expenditures, review of line-item programs, and other funding issues. The key is selecting the "right" member of Congress, usually at the subcommittee or committee chair level, and to make the right request relative to the department or rule in question. These reports and investigations can significantly affect Congress's authorization and appropriations process.

The Funding Level of Departments and Agencies

Federal government departments and agencies respond to budget considerations for their various programs throughout the year. They are protective of their funding requests to Congress and guard their presentations to the Office of Management and Budget (OMB) requesting administration support for this project or deletion of that project. Agencies strive to foster good relations with members of committees that formulate their budgets and oversee their operations.

Government relations professionals can influence funding levels in the federal government through the congressional legislative process, most notably within the House and Senate Appropriations and Budget Committees, as they consider fiscal-year appropriations bills and budget resolutions. "Zeroing out" entire bureaus and functions within agencies for policy reasons and increasing the budget for a specific program to enhance the involvement of an industry or group are some of a broad scope of activities that can be initiated at the congressional level to affect agency funding or rulemaking activities.

Legislation and the Congressional Legislative Process

Whether the issue is a free-standing bill or an amendment to an appropriations bill to be considered by Congress, agency rulemaking and policies in the executive branch can be influenced and directed in one way or another. For example, many provisions in legislation direct an agency to stop a particular rulemaking, speed it up, or initiate the rule in a particular policy direction. Congress has passed amendments that are so specific that they refer to agency rulemaking by docket number or to a rule published in a specific *Federal Register* citation.

Another technique to influence the legislative process is to pass an amendment that limits the use of funds appropriated by Congress to implement a particular rule or policy. These operative legislative phrases usually begin: "None of the funds appropriated by this Act shall be used for…." Agencies also can be used to support legislation that is being considered for introduction or has been introduced, because their support frequently can mean the difference between passage and defeat for the bill. Many ranking members of Congress on committees (notably the chairs of subcommittees and committees) seek federal department or agency positions on legislation, and that position is key to achieving the desired outcome.

Congressional Inquiry and "Pressure"

Congressional oversight is universally recognized by federal government decision makers as an important tool to affect rulemaking or administration policy. Government relations professionals should submit targeted questions to be asked of government witnesses before congressional committees during the public hearing process. These questions may elicit answers to policy decision making.

Congressional letters to agencies inquiring about policies, interpretation of rules, or the promulgation of rules can be significant if sent by a combination of ranking chairpersons of subcommittees that have authorization or appropriations over the agency in question. Often, letters will be signed by many members of Congress who span the ideological spectrum or by a particular state congressional delegation that will be affected by the particular regulation or government policy. Federal officials, especially appointed high-level executive branch employees, tend to respond to political pressures from Capitol Hill if these efforts are specially targeted and coordinated.

Office of Management and Budget Presentations

OMB is directly involved in the review of rules, budgets, programs, and rulemaking. OMB assigns a specialist to each department, agency, bureau, and program to maintain on-going reviews of the entity's fiscal year submissions for program funding and other requirements. OMB is viewed by many as the "traffic cop" for the federal government and plays a critical role in developing internal, administrative oversight of programs, legislation, policy positions, and so forth.

Meetings with OMB officials responsible for the department or agency involved are critical to the overall government relations strategy. OMB also is involved in implementing many recently passed laws, such as the Paperwork Reduction Act and the Reg-Flex Act. This OMB review process can be a significant factor in determining whether agencies are conforming to congressional intent as required by the law in implementing rules through their internal agency process.

Use of the Media

Effective use of media within the broader government relations strategy is an important factor to consider in a rulemaking proceeding. Examples of this include a well-placed, widely read story in a national newspaper or magazine that publicizes an agency rulemaking decision about to be released and an article or opinion editorial that challenges an agency's rulemaking or policy initiative.

Public Comments and Hearings

During the public comment period of rulemaking, many groups organize letter-writing campaigns from organizations and individuals that would be affected by the rule. Some of these campaigns are aimed at flooding the agency with public sentiment on the policy. Some campaigns involve correspondence that are detailed and technical and reflect the industry's desire to influence the regulatory process.

In addition to generating public comments, associations should consider providing expert witnesses to testify at a public hearing. These hearings can mirror those on Capitol Hill in which written testimony is presented, questions are asked by federal officials running the hearing, and media advisories are made on the statements issued by a particular group.

Summary

Lobbying the federal government is a complex and involved process. Government relations professionals who must "walk the halls" of the agencies to present policy or rulemaking positions must be aware of many complex rules and regulations. To be effective, government relations professionals need to know the law, the regulatory process, and the rules involved in their areas of concern.

Selected Laws and U.S. Code Citations

- Freedom of Information Act, 5 U.S.C. 552
- Government in the Sunshine Act, 5 U.S.C. 552b
- Regulatory Flexibility Act, 5 U.S.C. 504
- Paperwork Reduction Act, P.L. 104-13
- Unfunded Mandates Reform Act, P.L. 104-4

State Government Relations

Dennis Brown, CAE

TODAY'S STATE GOVERNMENTS demand the attention of associations and professional societies on an ever-widening range of topics, many of which were formerly associated with the federal government. More than 100,000 bills are introduced annually in the fifty state legislatures. This challenge increases with the realization that there is no cookie-cutter means of examining the legislative and regulatory processes in the states. Each state has varied procedures and differing cultures. Legislative committees dealing with identical issues will have dissimilar names from one state to another, or issues may be assigned to committees that, at first glance, would not appear to have jurisdiction. The rules are different in each state and must be approached on a state-by-state basis.

National associations must face the fact that their staff, although well tested in the halls of Congress, may be unprepared for state government affairs. Working with layers of congressional staff and federal bureaucracy can be dramatically different from one-on-one discussions with state legislators who may not have an office or staff. The quick pace of state action without delays stemming from bureaucracy or administrative staff can appear like the speed of light compared with congressional deliberations on similar topics.

Legislative Procedures

As with the Congress, most associations will likely find their bills originating in the lower House and proceeding through committees to floor action before passage to the Senate. (The unicameral Nebraska legislature is an obvious exception.) Although the printed procedures of a state legislature designate a deadline for action by the House in order to allow consideration in the Senate, these parameters are easily circumvented if the bill is important to leadership. The variations among states mean national associationyour staff must learn the ropes over and over, from one state capital to another.

These differences in legislative procedures may make protecting your interests difficult, especially if a national association intends to provide a hands-on presence. State legislatures are laboratories of democracy, if not efficiency, and they operate on short schedules. To use time, personnel, and finances wisely, you must establish priorities. Generally speaking, state legislatures meet for 90 to 120 days within the first six months of the year. Some meet for as little as 30 to 60 days per year; bills can move within a week from introduction, through committees, to a floor vote. The combined legislative sessions that each state holds each year amounts to more than 200 months of legislative activity annually, not including special sessions.

When legislative sessions end, the interim study committees undertake critical review of issues to allow expedient consideration when the legislature returns the following year. These deliberations often take place just under the radar of tracking mechanisms put in place by national associations and societies. The legislation that emerges from these study committees can be very difficult to amend during the brief regular session of a state legislature. It is important to obtain a list of activities assigned to committees during adjournment.

National Meetings

States share information with one another to a greater extent than many in the private sector realize. This explains the advent of national trends on common issues in state legislatures. From the viewpoint of state governments, sharing intelligence streamlines the task of undertaking research of similar topics.

Examination of issues is facilitated by nationwide organizations representing state officials. Prominent examples include the National Conference of State Legislatures, Denver, Colorado (telephone: 303/830-2200; Washington office telephone: 202/624-5400); American Legislative Exchange Council, Washington, D.C. (telephone: 202/466-3800); and Council of State Governments, Lexington, Kentucky (telephone: 606/244-8000; Washington office telephone: 202/624-5460). To maximize your effectiveness, become an active participant at their meetings. Another resource for multi-state monitoring and lobbying of legislation through networking and liaison opportunities with state legislators is the State Government Affairs Council in Washington, D.C. (telephone: 202/728-0500).

Developing Association Resources

Resources devoted to state government relations should match the expectations given members of the industry or profession. Many national associations provide brief descriptions of state legislation in a publication that is managed without having to add to staff. This can be accomplished by subscribing to a computerized bill-tracking service accessed via modem. StateNet in Sacramento, California (telephone: 916/444-0840; Washington office telephone: 202/342-3950) is one such company offering bill introductions and updates on activity in all 50 states. Enhanced reports relating to legislative activity of concern to your industry or profession is available from firms such as Multistate Associates, Alexandria, Virginia (telephone: 703/684-1110) and State-side Associates, Arlington, Virginia (telephone: 703/525-7466).

It is a laborious task to track and directly lobby committee action on a multistate basis. Before tackling this task, consider the staff time necessary to deliver this member service. Promising a physical presence of national association staff in a state capital means hiring additional staff and dedicating more resources. Your budget will need to absorb several full-time staff and the required travel expenditures.

Partners and Priorities

National associations must involve state and local organizations in addition to allied professions when instituting a state government relations program. Many state association executives suffer from the consequences of national staff interfering in state capitals without prior notice. This is because national staff sometimes are condescending to state association executives, treating them as if they are unable to comprehend legislative strategy. Conversely, some state capital contacts can be overly suspicious of lobbyists from out-of-state. The resulting conflicts can be resolved if each respects the opinions and professional responsibilities of the other.

Anticipate that state lobbyists have made compromises, trade-offs, and commitments to legislators. You must become familiar with these agreements to function effectively. Your credibility will disappear if state legislators believe national staff are backing out of previous commitments made by the state association. State associations, lobbyists, and local members can alert the national office to these potential problems. If your industry does not have state associations, touch base with other organizations, such as the state Chamber of Commerce or other business and industry lobbying organizations. Many of them will be willing to share time and information to make your efforts in their state meaningful.

An effective state legislative program must prioritize issues to guarantee the wise use of member dues. Know which issues warrant staff travel to a state capital and which issues have lower priorities and require only timely notice in a member publication.

Volunteer Training

Volunteer members often have a limited amount of time to devote to federal and state government relations. If possible, develop a cadre of volunteers separate from those handling contacts with Congress. Surveys can help to identify association members who are willing to serve as state legislative coordinators. Train these coordinators in the unique aspects of state government relations. Your program may differ from those of allied organizations within the same industry, but it will be seen as strengthening the overall effort.

Few industries or professions can rely on volunteer coordinators as their primary source of information regarding activities in the state capital. Volunteers usually look to the association or society office for guidance. Networking with allied state organizations can be useful in accomplishing this task. However, volunteers should be given a plan of action that includes deadlines and a list of responsibilities.

The national association board of directors and executive committee members are key components in the network of volunteer coordinators. These leaders should be willing to endorse the concepts and information provided to the grassroots member base. They should know the issues well enough to address local gatherings.

Hiring a Lobbyist

Many national association executives have an unrealistic expectation of the costs associated with retaining lobbyists in state capitals. One result is sticker shock as they rush to employ a lobbyist during a legislative emergency. Whether retaining lobbyists on a permanent or emergency basis, investigate the cost in your key states before drafting a budget for state government relations. In major industrial states the cost may exceed your congressional outlays. You could consider sharing the expense of a lobbyist with members in the state unable to bear the entire cost. Shop and compare national firms offering lobbyists in every state; obtain recommendations from sources within a state. You may even find that lobbyists endorsed by contacts in the state can be retained for less through a company such as Multistate Associates of Alexandria, Virginia.

It is generally advisable to retain a lobbyist by fixed fee, payable in regular equal monthly amounts, either for the legislative session or as a continuous year-round retainer. Open-ended hourly fee arrangements can lead to unintended escalation of expenses and a strained relationship between the parties. Many consider a retainer dependent on degree of success, with a nominal payment in event of failure— a questionable practice. In some states, such an arrangement may draw attention from regulators. It is a fee agreement that should be avoided.

Do not expect a lobbyist to be an expert in your industry. When you hire a lobbyist, you are after access more than knowledge of your trade. Nonetheless, be certain the lobbyist has a basic understanding of your industry or profession. Instruct the lobbyist to coordinate with your grassroots members, state associations, and allied organizations. To avoid obvious conflicts with other clients represented by the firm, check the lobbyist's list of clients before signing on the dotted line. Don't tie the lobbyist down writing reports, as it only keeps them away from the trade for which they are retained. You want them in the halls of the legislature and not behind a keyboard. Finally, be certain the lobbyist has the ear of policy makers key to your issue.

Monitoring Legislation

As previously mentioned, computerized tracking of state legislative and regulatory issues is available. Many firms offer enhanced services complete with analysis. Several of these companies were listed earlier under Developing Association Resources. However, if your association is seeking proactive programs with a hands-on presence in states, remember that these services are not substitutes for direct action by association staff.

Issue Management

Managing issues in state legislation from the vantage point of a national office may involve factors that are not encountered when shepherding congressional activity. For example, does the position taken by in-state industry match out-of-state views? If your association members are subsidiaries, do the parent companies and their state government affairs personnel concur with your activity in the state?

What is the opinion of state associations relating to your positions on the issues? Speaking bluntly, a state association and in-state industry members may have bigger fish to fry than legislation deemed critical by national association and industry representatives from out-of-state. Don't assume they automatically agree with your priorities.

After learning the ropes in a state capital, don't allow backseat drivers at the national office to force a counterproductive strategy on you. Long-distance commentaries regarding strategy absent knowledge of events in the state can prove damaging to your interests. Demands to institute a strategy you know to be destructive can force some hard choices.

State Legislative Meetings

National associations can act as resources and behind-the-scenes facilitators of meetings between industry members and state policy makers. Meetings may be most productive if held at a member's facility located in the district of a key state legislator. Attendees may include all members who live or work in the legislative district or surrounding area, as well as other individuals identified from surveys as having social or business relationships with the legislator. Meetings in the state capital are particularly useful when legislation of concern is being considered. Your lobbyist or state association can facilitate a meeting request from association members in districts represented by legislators holding sway over the legislation.

Inviting state legislators to tour member facilities is an important means of educating public officials on your issues. A member volunteer coordinator should invite elected and executive branch officials to tour a local facility. Members of the state association and your lobbyist also should be invited. Encourage your volunteer leadership and state association executive to take charge of meetings conducted at the local level, with support from national staff.

Testimony

National association staff can help prepare members and affiliates for hearings. Before a hearing, national staff can research data to be given to the legislators, offer position papers printed on a state organization's letterhead, provide economic studies and informative handouts, and identify witnesses and experts who can brief state members on the issue. Practice sessions before hearings can also draw on the experience of national staff. The lessons learned in other states can be invaluable.

Regulatory Agencies

As on the federal level, the battle is not over when a bill is signed into law. Victory in the legislature can be lost in the regulatory agencies. Even well-intended regulations can harm industry if agencies fail to use commonly accepted terminology. Also, some states grant agencies extraordinary power to formulate rules in areas where no legislation exists, often under the guise of "keeping old laws up-to-date with new technology."

State regulators have national organizations through which regulations issued in one state are distributed to others. Therefore, national association and society staff often must protect the industry or profession from this eventuality by tracking the comment period for proposed regulations, the procedure for requesting a public hearing, and particulars of the appeals process. Procedural differences between states make these tasks difficult. Agency hearings often are conducted by agency officials who authored the proposed regulations. Be certain that your testimony, either oral or written, contains facts and figures to buttress their reasoning or point to a more appropriate approach.

Not all state agencies in every state follow the procedures recommended in the Model Administrative Procedure Act, which offers the public a chance to submit data or views in writing or testimony on proposed rules. In some states, rules established by a state regulatory agency receive superficial review by the legislature. You may be able to use this process to block unfavorable regulations.

Statewide Office Holders

You may consider establishing a direct relationship with statewide elected officials. This can be achieved on a state-by-state basis or through involvement with a variety of national organizations. The

National Governors Association (telephone: 202/624-5300) and the Federation of Tax Administrators (telephone: 202/624-5890) are both located in the Hall of the States at 444 New Jersey Avenue, Washington, D.C., while the National Association of Attorneys General (telephone: 202/326-6000) can be found at 750 First Street, N.E., Washington, D.C. Each is an example of an organization representing state executive branch officials. Moreover, the National Conference of State Legislatures and Council of State Governments administer a wide variety of organizations representing legislative and executive branch officials.

Register as a Lobbyist

Dennis Brown, CAE

The states have a patchwork of laws that regulate contacts with legislative and executive branch officials. Even just talking to state legislators and legislative or executive staff before registering as a lobbyist is a violation of the law in some states. Buying lunch for a state legislator is forbidden in some states but permissible without reporting requirements in others. Check the law before you lobby in a state. *State Lobbying Laws* (published by State & Federal Communications; telephone: 330/836-3600) is one resource to keep abreast of changing and various lobbying laws.

No Members in the State

Special challenges await national associations venturing into states with no industry members. One way to overcome hurdles is to network with state associations and lobbyists representing allied organizations. Employing a lobbyist is another method of effecting a quick response to fast-breaking events in a state where your association does not have members. Touching base with statewide business groups, such as the Chamber of Commerce, can help your association staff learn the ropes and avoid mine fields.

Municipalities

Fully engage your state government program before tackling the kaleidoscope of conditions and personalities to be found in municipal government. Difficulties to be surmounted in the fifty state legislatures can appear tame compared to the thousands of local government units across the nation. Organizations such as the National Association of Counties, Washington, D.C. (telephone: 202/393-

6226) and National League of Cities, Washington, D.C. (telephone: 202/626-3000) can be helpful.

Summary

State association executives and grassroots industry members are the key to establishing an effective state government relations program from the national headquarters of an association or professional society. Learn what they expect from the national office and promise only what can be delivered. For instance, a state association may look to the national office for monetary support, but you may have forty-nine other states also demanding a portion of your limited resources. Develop nonmonetary assistance that will serve the interests of many states. A coordinated program that promotes the exchange of valuable knowledge and essential information will develop an effective defense against unwanted legislation while promoting favorable laws.

National, state, and local industry representatives must speak with one voice. Share information to be certain your talking points are consistent, regardless of the source. Show the respect you expect to receive. Mutual respect is the most important ingredient to a winning combination.

Lobbying Local Governments More Effectively

Michelle K. Brooks

Why Do You Want to Lobby at the Local Level?

Lobbying at the local level provides an association or industry group with a variety of important opportunities. First of all, it allows an association to exercise greater control over its issues and to see more immediate results. Issues are usually more manageable at the local level because of the limited number of players. There are four basic groups: the elected officials; the community leaders; the media (local press); and the citizens. Secondly, the local level can be used as a forum or proving ground to test your association's strategies and talking points in support of or opposition to a given position. You will be able to quickly see which arguments sell and which do not serve your purpose. Finally, it gives your association the ability to develop relationships with local elected officials who often have higher political aspirations. These relationships can easily last for years and continue into all levels of government.

How Local Governments are Organized

Local governments generally consist of a small body of elected officials. The number varies depending on the size of the community (i.e., five, seven, or nine individuals). It is usually an odd number, with one member serving as the mayor or chair. The leadership position can be directly elected or rotate among the body with a vote of their peers. These officials are typically elected to four-year, staggered terms.

The elected body is supported by a city staff that can be comprised of both paid and volunteer positions, such as a city administrator or manager, a city clerk, a city attorney, a planning department, a parks and recreation department, or a community redevelopment agency. The number of departments and agencies as well as the paid staff is always determined by the size of the city or township, the financial condition of the community, and the unique industries or features of a particular community. For example, a town with a large senior population may have a department that caters specifically to seniors' needs.

Other Structural Aspects of Local Governments

Just like their federal and state counterparts, local governments have a variety of committees or commissions set up to review and screen community issues. Often times the issues are brought before these bodies for a recommendation before they face the local elected officials. Citizens are appointed to these positions and normally serve as volunteers. Again, depending on the size of the community and its budget, some of these positions may be paid. If volunteers, they may receive a monthly stipend or some kind of reimbursement for out-of-pocket expenses. The commission or committee that handles planning and zoning issues is usually the most powerful (outside of the elected body). If someone is seeking public recognition in hopes of running for a city-elected position, he or she will usually seek an appointment to the planning commission.

Public Officials in Local Politics

Local elected officials are more easily accessible than those at any other level of government. This is because you do not have to go through staff to obtain access, and the elected officials *want* to be available to their constituents (a very common campaign promise). They often offer their home telephone numbers and welcome calls after normal business hours…within reason! Many local elected officials hold other jobs outside of their positions and serve the community on a voluntary basis, just as commissioners or committee members. This means the backgrounds of those who serve on the council can be quite diverse. The body may be elected from the city as a whole or they may be elected to represent a specific geographic region or district.

Local political campaigns are normally grassroots oriented and usually encompass a short campaign season. An association will find that becoming involved and ultimately influencing the local elections can be relatively easy once you know the lay of the land and the key community players. It is always better for an association or outside organization to work through an existing community group or a key community leader. An organization that enters the local political scene with too big a splash (i.e., lots of money or extremely slick literature) can face some harmful political fallout. Some cities or towns may have campaign spending limits and advertising regulations. You will want to check with the city clerk to see if any of these apply before entering the campaign arena.

Monitoring Local Government Activities

A city council or local elected body will usually meet twice a month. One way to monitor a city's activities is to receive copies of the council agendas through the mail. In the state of California, for instance, cities are required to post an agenda seventy-two hours before a council meeting. So if the agenda is mailed to you, it might arrive after the meeting. To avoid missing an important issue, you may want to regularly call the city clerk. The city clerk and various departments are also repositories of committee reports and background materials. These can often be obtained prior to the council meetings; sometimes there is a small fee. The typical council agenda is comprised of resolutions, ordinances, new business, old business, and public comment. An ordinance is the most binding of the actions a council can take. Ordinances are laws that become part of the municipal code and require both a first and second reading (basically a public hearing) before a final vote can be taken. If the ordinance is substantially amended during the first reading, the council must repeat the first reading process. Most public testimony is taken during the first reading.

How You Can Best Influence Local Government Decisions

If you know you have an issue that will come before the city council, the first course of action is to meet with each of the elected officials. Provide the council members with as much factual information as possible and as early as possible. Some states may have laws that prohibit meeting with more than one elected official at once, so be sure and find out what the meeting policies are.

If your time is limited, submit your position paper to the city clerk prior to the council meeting so it will become a part of the record. At the council meeting, testimony is always welcome from the audience, yet time may be limited by the council. The length of time usually depends on the subject matter, the community's interest, and the number of citizens attending the meeting who want to speak. If you have not had time to meet with each council member, at least now they will see that the issue was important enough for you to testify in person. When you deliver your public testimony, be specific and address concerns that may have come up during your meetings. Always mention that you have submitted written testimony to the city clerk and avoid making legal threats. Local elected officials take a strong dislike to threats of legal action.

If you support the council on an item, give them as much help as possible in seeing the virtues of voting with you. If you oppose an issue, either you can recommend any of a number of actions to defeat the measure or obtain something more acceptable. Getting one of the council members to refer an item to a committee or special task force is one method of diverting it. Another is raising major concerns in the ordinance that the city is proposing, thereby creating the need for a second first reading. If the ordinance needs to be reviewed by the city attorney, this will buy you time to meet with the council members and raise support among the community.

As with any level of government advocacy, the more education you provide and the greater lead time you give, the better the chances of success.

Adding the Courts to Your Lobbying Arsenal: A Case Study

Andrew C. Briscoe III

MOTHERS AGAINST DRUNK DRIVING (MADD), a 501(c)(3) organization, faced two major judicial opportunities in a five-year period that helped to advance its mission to stop drunk driving and establish opportunities for future support.

MADD's key objectives to lobbying and influencing judicial output were to secure an appropriate candidate to sit on the highest court in the nation, which makes decisions on the laws offenders will be accountable to, and to protect the legal avenues with which it achieves its mission.

Influencing Judicial Appointments

One area MADD targeted was the appointment of federal judicial officials, specifically Supreme Court justices. In most political situations or elections, a 501(c)(3) nonprofit organization is not allowed to lobby for or against a particular candidate. However, federal political appointments are not included in the rule. Therefore, associations that determine a particular federal judicial candidate is potentially favorable to their mission or cause can request to testify in support of the candidate.

A judicial candidate's views can be researched in several ways, including via the Internet through specialized services that include LEXIS-NEXIS and Westlaw. Research of cases the candidate has been involved in and the resulting rulings can be revealing.

MADD's involvement in the chief justice selection process was prefaced by several questions: Should MADD support a Supreme Court nominee? Should it oppose a nominee? Should MADD choose to stay neutral and not testify? Or should it choose to submit written testimony in support or in opposition? These questions challenged MADD's decision makers, including volunteers and staff.

Leadership's ultimate decision to testify was influenced by a call from the White House. The administration wanted a female-oriented group to testify in support of now Supreme Court Justice Souter. MADD reviewed Souter's previous rulings and found that out of the more than one hundred cases he had ruled on, more than ten were directly or indirectly related to drunk driving, and a majority of these rulings were favorable to MADD's mission.

However, it is not always wise to get involved in supporting or opposing a federal appointee. For example, MADD chose not to testify in support of or in opposition to sitting Supreme Court Justice Clarence Thomas. After reviewing the rulings Thomas had issued before becoming a nominee to the Supreme Court, MADD leaders felt that Thomas's past rulings had no direct effect for or against MADD's mission. Even though the White House again had requested MADD's involvement, MADD decided not to participate in the hearings.

Because the White House gives relatively short notice when a judicial nominee is proposed, associations may need to decide quickly whether or not to testify. Associations may have only a few weeks to solicit outside volunteer support to make the testimony happen or to have staff research and draft testimony. Testimony should be coordinated with collaborating supporters to ensure that different supporting perspectives are presented.

Influencing Litigation

Another area your organization can focus on is the use of *amicus curiae,* also know as *amicus* briefs or "friend of the court" briefs. MADD submitted to the Supreme Court an *amicus* brief related to sobriety checkpoints—a drunk-driving tool used to target the offender. Attorneys working with the American Civil Liberties Union (ACLU) in Michigan had filed a case claiming sobriety checkpoints were unconstitutional and infringed on driver's privacy rights.

The legal standing of the attorneys was challenged because none of them had actually driven through a sobriety checkpoint. The attorneys claimed they had valid Michigan driver's licenses and, therefore, were potentially subject to such intrusions at Michigan sobriety checkpoints.

When the case reached the U.S. Supreme Court, MADD chose to submit an *amicus* brief. In fact, MADD attempted to circumvent the Supreme Court standard, which allows only one *amicus* brief from each entity or organization submitting. The Michigan Chapter of MADD submitted one brief, and a second brief was submitted from the national office; the Supreme Court allowed and accepted both briefs.

Through *amicus* briefs, MADD was able to state its case without being directly involved in the court case; the actual case was between the ACLU attorneys and the State of Michigan. MADD was not a defendant, but it became involved in the issue because the case was directly related to MADD's cause.

On the day MADD filed the *amicus* brief, it held a press conference to ensure that the general public would be made aware of the case to go before the court and MADD's position. Associations that choose to submit an *amicus* brief should consider a public relations element, with some media exposure to help bring the issue out. Association leaders should also make themselves available to the media immediately after the hearing on the Supreme Court steps. Finally, once a ruling is issued, make use of yet another public relations opportunity if the ruling is favorable.

The most costly position in litigation is being the defendant. As an outside party, your association will have better leverage and can take advantage of the additional public relations potential without appearing to influence the court. Associations can limit their potential exposure by being a sideline or indirect participant. Associations should pick and choose their involvement; you should only become involved in cases that stand a good chance of producing a positive outcome for your association and its members or industry.

In preparing *amicus* briefs, volunteer legal support is critical, especially if your organization has limited resources. Associations may need to ask a law firm to contribute its time and resources.

Another critical element is research. MADD researched cases dealing with sobriety checkpoints and researched profiles of the Supreme Court justices and how they might approach the hearing of the case. Using this information, staff and volunteer legal counsel drafted and submitted the brief.

Getting Involved in the Judicial Process

An association interested in being involved in the judicial process should create a vision of its ability to influence the judicial process; the process should not be considered a sideline objective. Associations should aggressively stay on top of issues of concern at the state levels because these cases may end up going to the Supreme Court. Educate your board to be aware of potential federal judicial opportunities. Keep in touch with the Senate committee responsible for hearings on federal nominees. These efforts will set the stage for a strong position when the next Supreme Court candidate is nominated or when issues that affect the association and its members or industry go before the U.S. Supreme Court.

The spokesperson for any public relations efforts relating to endorsing a Supreme Court candidate or submitting an *amicus* brief should be the president or chair of the association. In any case, the spokesperson should be someone approved by the board or executive committee, because this person will be representing the organization publicly and legally. Volunteer legal support should be available to respond to legal questions with which the spokesperson may not be familiar.

Funding Options

Funding options are not always clear cut. Legal counsel usually is the most expensive part of litigation. In some cases, an attorney or law firm will volunteer legal services in exchange for the publicity the involvement may bring. Travel and public relations expenses also need to be considered. A 501(c)(6) association may seek contributions into an informal coalition fund to help defer cost.

If an association selects its judicial involvements carefully and does its homework, its investment in the process will reap many benefits. MADD's support of Souter helped to gain an influential ally in its fight against drunk driving. In the Michigan case on sobriety checkpoints, the court ultimately ruled favorably in support of the checkpoints.

An Introduction to Congressional Procedures

Michael E. Kastner

All Legislative Powers herein granted shall be vested in a Congress of the United States, which shall consist of a Senate and House of Representatives.

– Article I, Section 1 of the U.S. Constitution

The Basics

The Senate is composed of 100 members, two from each state. A U.S. senator must be at least thirty years old, have been a U.S. citizen for at least nine years, and have been a resident of the state from which the senator is chosen when elected. A senator's term of office is six years, with one-third of the Senate membership elected every two years. Each senator has one vote.

The U.S. House of Representatives is composed of 435 members, all of whom are elected every two years. The 435 seats are apportioned among the fifty states according to population. A representative must be at least twenty-five years old, have been a citizen of the United States for at least seven years, and have been a resident of the state from which the representative was chosen when elected. Each representative has one vote.

In addition to the 435 representatives in the House, there is a resident commissioner from the Commonwealth of Puerto Rico and delegates from the District of Columbia, American Samoa, Guam, and the Virgin Islands. The resident commissioner and delegates are allowed to vote in the Committee of the Whole (see section on Committee of the Whole), but such votes are subject to revotes by the House if their votes may have been decisive.

A Congress lasts for two years, beginning in January following the election of members. A Congress is divided into two one-year sessions.

The primary function of Congress is to debate and enact legislation. Only the House may initiate revenue bills, while the Senate has the power of advice and consent with regard to treaties and nominations.

How It Gets Started

Congressional action starts with the introduction of a proposal in one of four principal forms: the bill, the joint resolution, the concurrent resolution, or the simple resolution.

Michael E. Kastner

Bills

A bill is the most common form of legislation. It can be permanent, temporary, general, special, public, or private. Most bills are public.

A bill originating in the House of Representatives is designated by the letters "H.R.," signifying House of Representatives, followed by a sequenced number based on the order of its introduction. Bills are sent to the president for action when approved in identical form by both the House of Representatives and the Senate. Once approved by the president, these bills become public or private law. Public laws affect the entire nation while private laws affect only an individual or specified group.

Joint Resolutions

Joint resolutions may originate in either chamber. There is little difference between a bill and a joint resolution. Both follow the same parliamentary road to becoming law, except that joint resolutions propose an amendment to the Constitution. In this case, such a resolution must be approved by two-thirds of both the House and Senate. Once approved by both chambers, it is sent directly to the administrator of general services for submission to the individual states for ratification instead of to the president. A joint resolution originating in the House of Representatives is designated "H.J.Res." followed by its individual number, and one introduced in the Senate is designated "S.J.Res."

Concurrent Resolutions

Matters affecting the operations of both the House of Representatives and Senate, such as creation of a joint committee, usually are initiated by means of concurrent resolutions. Concurrent resolutions also are used to express the sense of the Congress to the president or other parties or to correct the language of measures passed by one chamber (an engrossment) or both chambers (an enrollment). A concurrent resolution from the House of Representatives is designated "H.Con.Res." followed by its individual number. Concurrent resolutions are not sent to the president for approval. Once approved by both the House of Representatives and Senate, they are signed by the clerk of the House and the secretary of the Senate.

Simple Resolutions

A matter concerning the operation of one chamber alone is initiated by a simple resolution. A resolution affecting the House of Representatives is designated "H.Res." followed by its number. These resolutions need to be approved only by the originating chamber and, like concurrent resolutions, are not sent to the president for action. Simple resolutions generally take care of housekeeping measures, such as changes to the rules of the House or Senate.

Introduction and Referral

Bills may be introduced in their respective chambers by any senator or member, the resident commissioner, and delegates of the House of Representatives. Both the House and Senate allow for unlimited numbers of sponsors for introduction of a bill (although, in the Senate, only one name will appear when reported). In the House, the bill to be introduced is placed in the "hopper" at the side of the clerk's desk, given a number, and then referred to the appropriate committee(s) by the speaker of the House with the assistance of the parliamentarian. Multiple committee referrals may be either concurrent or sequential. In the Senate, the bill usually is presented to the clerks at the presiding officer's desk. A senator also may rise and introduce the bill from the floor. If any senator objects to the introduction, it is delayed until the next day. If there is no objection, the Senate bill or resolution is read by title and referred to the appropriate committee by the parliamentarian in the name of the vice president, who sits as the president of the Senate.

The House of Representatives

Committee Action

Every committee has jurisdiction over matters and measures affecting a given area of law. Legislation affecting those areas are referred to those committees. Legislation may be referred to multiple committees. Committees are made up of members from each party. The proportion of party members on a committee is determined by the majority party (except the Standards and Official Conduct Committee, which is equally divided). A committee member's rank in seniority is based on the date of his or her committee appointment. Until recently, the committee chair was the senior-ranking majority member of the committee. Now, House rules require that committee chairs be elected from nominations submitted by the majority party caucus.

Most committees have at least two subcommittees; House standing committees with more than 20 members must have at least four subcommittees. Each committee has professional and clerical staff.

Once a bill has been referred to a committee, the chair has two weeks to refer it to the appropriate subcommittee unless a majority of the majority party members vote to consider the bill in full committee.

Committee and Subcommittee Hearings

If a bill is sufficiently important, the committee or subcommittee may set a date for a public hearing. Hearings must be announced at least one week in advance, unless the committee has good cause for holding it sooner. Committee and subcommittee hearings are public unless committee members vote in open session to close a hearing, typically for national security reasons. Hearings on the budget are required to be held by the Appropriations Committee within thirty days of its transmittal to Congress.

Hearings are transcribed. After introductory remarks by the members of the committee, witnesses are called. Representatives or senators wishing to testify typically are called first as a courtesy. Witnesses generally are required to file with the committee some written statement or outline of their testimony in advance. House committee rules allow each member five minutes to question a witness. The hearing transcript is made available by the committee when completed.

Subcommittee Action

Once hearings are complete, the subcommittee or committee will likely hold a mark-up session. The views of both sides are debated, and ultimately a vote is taken. If in subcommittee, the subcommittee may decide to report the bill favorably to the full committee, with or without amendments, or table the bill (postpone indefinitely).

Committee Action

Reports from subcommittees are made to the full committee and discussed or amended. A vote of the committee determines whether the bill is reported favorably to the House or tabled. If reported favorably, the bill may be amended or sent clean. The committee may decide to report a new bill that incorporates its amendments (technically, the new bill is introduced, often by the committee chair, referred to the committee, and reported favorably by the committee). It is unusual but nonetheless possible for a committee to report a bill unfavorably or without a recommendation. Generally, a committee will just table a bill if it wants to kill it.

Reported Bills

Once a bill is reported favorably to the House, a committee member is chosen to write the committee report. The report details the scope of the bill and reasons for the committee's approval. At the time of committee approval, a member may give notice that he or she intends to file supplemental, minority, or additional views to the committee report. Once completed, the committee report is filed with the House.

The bill is reprinted when reported, with committee amendments indicated by italics and deletions by line-through type. A report number and calendar number are added to the newly printed bill. If the bill was referred to multiple committees in sequence, the calendar number is printed when the final sequential committee has completed its work. The calendar number is from either the Union Calendar or House Calendar.

Calendars

The rules of the House provide that there must be:

First. A Calendar of the Committee of the Whole House on the state of the Union, to which shall be referred bills raising revenue, general appropriation bills and bills of a public character directly or indirectly appropriating money or property.

This is the Union Calendar, and most public bills being reported to the House are placed on it.

Second. A House Calendar, to which shall be referred all bills of a public character not raising revenue nor directly or indirectly appropriating money or property.

This is the House calendar.

In the past, if a measure pending on either the House or Union Calendars was noncontroversial, it could be placed on the Consent Calendar. In recent years, unanimous consent and suspension of the rules has effectively taken the place of the Consent Calendar (see section on Corrections Calendar).

There also exists a Private Calendar. Private bills are referred to the Private Calendar. This calendar is called on the first and third Tuesday of each month. If objection is made by two or more members, the bill is recommitted to committee.

Corrections Calendar

In 1995 the House replaced the Consent Calendar with the Corrections Calendar. The Consent Calendar was originally created as a way to expedite action on noncontroversial measures. It had fallen into disuse because of the increased use of unanimous consent and suspension of the rules in the House. In the 102nd and 103rd Congresses, no bills were brought up on the Consent Calendar.

The House created the Corrections Calendar to expedite or repeal laws, regulations, or rules that are, in the opinion of the House, obsolete, burdensome, or duplicative.

Only bills favorably reported from committees and assigned to either the House or Union Calendars are eligible for the Corrections Calendar. The speaker places bills on the Corrections Calendar in consultation with the minority leader and a bipartisan Corrections Day Advisory Group, made up of seven Republicans and five Democrats.

The speaker may call the Corrections Calendar on the second and fourth Tuesdays of each month. Bills must be on the Corrections Calendar for at least three (legislative) days before they may be taken up.

Corrections Day bills are debated for one equally divided hour. Amendments are not in order under the five-minute rule. Only amendments offered by the chair of the primary committee or authorized by that committee are in order during the one-hour period.

A three-fifths vote is required to pass bills brought to the floor via the Corrections Calendar. Any bill that fails to attract the three-fifths majority remains on its original Calendar and continues to be eligible for floor consideration under other House procedures.

The Rules Committee

Bills are given calendar numbers in sequence, but some bills are more important than others. These bills can be taken out of order by grant of a special resolution or rule from the Rules Committee. The rule may waive points of order against the bill. The rule also may limit or prevent floor amendments. This is known as a closed rule.

Motion to Discharge

A member may petition to discharge a committee from consideration of a bill. This petition is presented to the clerk and must then be signed by a majority of the total House membership. Once a majority signs on, the bill is placed on the Calendar of Motions to Discharge Committees.

On the second and fourth Monday a member may call up a bill that has been on this Calendar for at least seven days. After twenty minutes of evenly divided debate, the House votes on the motion to discharge. The member may then move for immediate consideration. If this motion is defeated, the bill moves to the proper calendar as if it had been reported favorably by the committee.

Motion to Suspend the Rules

On Monday and Tuesday of each week, and during the last six days of a session, motions to suspend the rules may be entertained. The motion must be seconded by a majority of the members present, unless the bill has been available for at least one full legislative day. The motion to suspend the rules and pass the bill is debated for forty evenly divided minutes. The motion may not be amended, and any amendments to the bill must be included in the motion. The rules may be suspended and the bill passed only by a two-thirds majority of those voting.

Calendar Wednesday

On Wednesday of each week in session, the standing committees are called and may bring up for consideration bills they have reported or that are on the House or Union Calendars. No more than two hours of general debate is allowed on a bill called up on Calendar Wednesday. A simple majority of those members present voting in the affirmative will pass the measure.

Privileged Matters

Certain privileged matters can interrupt the standard order of business. Rules Committee reports or Appropriations Committee reports on general appropriations bills are considered privileged matters. Other privileged matters include conference reports and veto messages from the president. Measures concerning the District of Columbia also may be privileged on certain days.

Privileged matters can, with certain detailed exceptions, be brought up for immediate consideration at any time. In practice, privileged matters generally are brought up only after consultation with the majority and minority floor leaders.

Floor Consideration

The House can act with a quorum of 100 members instead of the requisite 218 when resolved into what is known as the Committee of the Whole House on the State of the Union, also known as the Committee of the Whole. The Committee of the Whole is a parliamentary procedure allowing the House to operate as a committee on which every member of the House serves. The Committee of the Whole operates under a somewhat different set of rules than the House, the purpose being to expedite the floor process, and considers all measures on the Union Calendar. This process is typically initiated by a rule from the Rules Committee, which fixes the length of debate. After the House adopts the rule, the House votes to resolve itself into the Committee of the Whole and proceeds with debate.

The placement of the sergeant of arms' mace—a column of ebony rods to the right of the Speaker—indicates whether the House or the Committee of the Whole is meeting. If the House is meeting, the rods are placed in a green marble pedestal. If the Committee of the Whole is meeting, the rods are placed in a white marble pedestal, which is positioned somewhat lower on the podium. Additionally, it is not the speaker who presides over the Committee of the Whole, but rather a designee who is addressed as Mr./Mrs./Ms. Chairman (as they now Chair the Committee of the Whole) rather than Mr. Speaker.

In the Committee of the Whole, bills are debated according to the Rules Committee resolution for the bill.

Second Reading

Once debate is completed, the bill is read a second time. At this point, a member may be allowed to speak for up to five minutes on amendments to the bill. An opponent also is allowed five minutes.

There is no further debate allowed. This is known as the five-minute rule and is designed to prevent filibusters.

The Committee Rises

After consideration, the Committee of the Whole rises and reports the bill to the House with any amendments that have been approved. At this point, the Committee of the Whole resolves back into the House. The House then acts on the bill and its amendments.

House Action

To close debate on a bill, a majority must move the previous question. If this motion carries, the speaker then asks if the bill should be read a third time. If this motion is approved by a majority of those voting, a vote on passage will occur. After voting on amendments, the House will vote on passage. After the previous question has been ordered, one motion to recommit the bill to a committee is allowed. This motion generally is not subject to debate, unless the motion is to recommit with instructions, in which case debate is allowed for between ten minutes and one hour.

If the previous question has not been ordered, the House may debate for one hour, and then the previous question is ordered, and the House votes on passage. Offering amendments during this debate is in order.

After passage, a motion to reconsider is automatically made and laid on the table. Laying the motion on the table postpones indefinitely action on the motion to reconsider.

Voting

There are four methods of voting, three applicable to the Committee of the Whole, and one additional method allowed in the House. The methods include voice vote, division, recorded vote, and the yeas and nays (used only in the House).

Generally, a voice vote is taken first. If this is inconclusive, a division may be demanded, and those in favor are asked to rise and be counted.

If a recorded vote is requested and supported by one-fifth of a quorum of the House or twenty-five members of the Committee of the Whole, the vote is taken by electronic device. Members usually have fifteen minutes in which to record their vote.

If the yeas and nays are demanded in the House, with approval of one-fifth of the members present, the clerk calls the roll, and each member answers aye or no. House rules strictly prohibit one member from casting a vote for another member.

Pairing of Members

If a member expects to be absent for a vote, he or she may arrange to be paired with another absent member who would have voted in an opposite manner. This pairing shows how the members would have voted. Pairs are not counted in determining the outcome of a vote but provide members an opportunity to express how they would have voted.

Bells and Lights

The Capitol and House and Senate Office Buildings are equipped with a system of bells and lights to notify members when they are needed for votes.

In the House

1 long ring followed by a pause and then 3 rings and 3 lights on the left means start or continuation of a notice or short quorum call in the Committee of the Whole that will be vacated if and when 100 members appear on the floor. Bells are repeated every five minutes unless the call is vacated or the call is converted into a regular quorum call.

1 long ring and extinguishing of 3 lights on the left means short or notice quorum call vacated.

2 rings and 2 lights on the left means recorded vote, yea-and-nay vote, or automatic roll call vote by electronic device. The bells are repeated five minutes after the first ring.

2 rings and 2 lights on the left, followed by a pause and then 2 more rings, means automatic roll call vote or yea-and-nay vote taken by a call of the roll in the House. The bells are repeated when the clerk reaches the R's in the first call of the roll.

2 rings followed by a pause and then 5 rings means first vote under Suspension of the Rules or on clustered votes. Two bells are repeated five minutes after the first ring. The first vote will take 15 minutes, with successive votes at intervals of not less than five minutes. Each successive vote is signaled by five rings.

3 rings and 3 lights on the left means regular quorum call in either the House or in the Committee of the Whole by electronic device or by clerks. The bells are repeated five minutes after the first ring.

3 rings followed by a pause and then 3 more rings means regular quorum call by a call of the roll. The bells are repeated when the clerk reaches the R's in the first call of the roll.

3 rings followed by a pause and then 5 more rings means a quorum call in the Committee of the Whole that may be followed immediately by a five-minute recorded vote.

4 rings and 4 lights on the left means adjournment of the House.

5 rings and 5 lights on the left means any five-minute vote.

6 rings and 6 lights on the left means recess of the House.

12 rings at 2-second intervals with 6 lights on the left is a civil defense warning.

The 7th light indicates that the House is in session.

In the Senate

The lights above the doors in the north side of the chamber and throughout the Senate complex correspond to a system of bells that alert Senators to such legislative activities as voting and quorum calls.

One long ring announces the opening of each day's session.

Four short rings signal the end of a daily session.

One short ring notifies Senators to return to the chamber for a yea-and-nay vote.

Five short rings warn that only seven and a half minutes remain for the vote.

A red light remains lit while the Senate is in session.

A bright lamp is also lit on the top of the Capitol dome to indicate when the Senate or House is meeting.

House Engrossment

Once the House has amended and passed a bill, it must be reprinted. This task can be more complicated than it may sound, as all amendments to the bill must be properly incorporated by the enrolling clerk.

The enrolling clerk serves under the Clerk of the House. This clerk gathers all papers relating to the bill and prepares an engrossed copy of the bill as agreed to by the House. At this point, the bill is technically an "Act" of the House rather than a bill, but it is still generally referred to as a bill.

The engrossed bill is printed on blue paper and certified by the Clerk of the House that it has passed the House. The engrossed bill is delivered by a reading clerk to the Senate.

The Senate

The Senate is designed to be the more deliberative of the two chambers. To this end, Senators have the right of extended debate (filibuster). As a result of this right to filibuster, the Senate rules encourage conducting business by consensus whenever possible. The Senate is also designed as a continuing body. Senatorial terms are six years long, and only one-third of the Senate's seats are up for election every two years, in contrast to the House, where every seat is up for election at every two-year election.

Bill Introduction

Bills are introduced by senators and referred to committees as indicated earlier. When the Senate receives a bill passed by the House, the bill is referred to the appropriate committee and reprinted. The reprinted bill is known as an "act print" or a "Senate referred print."

Committee Action

Senate committees act on bills in the same manner as House committees. They may report the bill with or without amendments, and reports are filed. As in the House, a Senator may file a minority or supplemental report. Committee-reported bills are reprinted in the same manner as House bills, with new words in italics and deleted words in line-through type. The Senate calendar and report numbers are printed on the bill once reported by committee.

Senate Chamber Procedure

Unanimous consent is the key to Senatorial procedure.

Once a bill is reported, the Majority Leader will ask unanimous consent for immediate consideration of the bill. If it is a noncontroversial bill and there is no objection, the bill may be passed with little or no debate by a simple majority vote. Amendments may also be adopted at this time with a simple majority vote. If there is objection to the unanimous consent request, the bill is placed on the Senate calendar after one legislative day. Bills reported by standing committees must have been available for at least two days prior to Senate consideration unless agreed to otherwise by the majority and minority leaders.

In addition to the simple unanimous consent request, bills may be brought up in the Senate by the Majority Leader via a very detailed unanimous consent agreement or by a motion to proceed.

A detailed unanimous consent agreement can also be called a time agreement and is similar to a rule from the House Rules Committee. It may limit debate and detail how the time is divided. It may also limit amendments to the measure.

A motion to proceed to the consideration of a measure on the calendar is typically made when a unanimous consent agreement cannot be reached.

Senate Calendars

The Senate has two calendars: the Calendar of Business and the Executive Calendar. All legislation is placed on the Business Calendar, while treaties and nominations are placed on the Executive Calendar.

At the conclusion of morning business for each legislative day, the Senate proceeds to consideration of the calendar. It is important to note that because morning business comes at the beginning of a new "legislative day" and the Senate often recesses instead of adjourning at the end of a day, a legislative day could actually last weeks or even months. Thus, there is rarely a call of the calendar. When it is called, bills not objected to are taken up in order.

Morning Hour and Morning Business

At the beginning of each daily session the Majority Leader, by unanimous consent, provides a brief period of time to go over the schedule for the day and any other matters of interest. A similar period of time is allotted to the Minority Leader.

During the morning hour of each legislative day, the Journal is read and messages, reports, and communications are laid before the Senate. Messages between the two chambers and messages from the president are also read.

The presiding officer then calls for presentations and memorials. Next, the presiding officer calls for committee reports and bill introductions.

Consideration of Measures on the Floor

Most measures in the Senate are passed either on the call of the calendar or by unanimous consent. Unanimous consent is typically preferred, as the consent agreement can spell out debate limitations. Motions to proceed to consideration of a measure on the calendar is typically made only when there has been an objection to a unanimous consent request.

Cloture may be required on controversial measures for which there is no unanimous consent agreement. Cloture is a tool typically used to end a filibuster. Cloture is invoked by three-fifths of the senators voting affirmatively to close debate. If the cloture vote is on a senate rule, a two-thirds affirmative vote is required.

Once cloture is invoked, further debate is limited to no more than one hour for each senator and 30 additional hours for consideration of the matter.

Senate Floor Voting

The Senate has several methods for voting on amendments or bills under consideration. These methods include voice votes, division, and the yeas and nays. The yeas and nays may be requested and will be ordered if seconded by one-fifth of a presumptive quorum (at least 11). The yeas and nays are constitutionally required in the case of a veto. Typically, the presiding officer will just assume such a quorum and simultaneously ring the bells signaling such a vote. The senators are then called alphabetically to register their vote. The Senate, like the House, also provides for "pairing" of votes to allow senators who know they will be absent to indicate how they would have voted.

Amending Senate Measures on the Floor

Bills before the Senate are subject to amendment. Committee amendments take priority (except committee substitutes, which always come last), then individual senators may offer amendments from the floor. During consideration of committee amendments, the only amendments from the floor in order would be amendments to the committee amendment. These are known as second-degree amendments. Once committee amendments are finished, any Senator can offer any amendments to the bill.

There are a few limits to the amendment process in the Senate. Amendments to amendments to amendments (which would be third-degree amendments) are not in order (although a second-degree amendment to the committee substitute, which is in effect a third-degree amendment, is allowable). Additionally, during consideration of general appropriations bills, amendments must be germane and not propose new general legislation or increase the amount of the appropriation unless previously authorized or estimated for in the president's budget.

Unanimous consent agreements also typically limit the amendment process. The agreement may require germaneness for amendments or limit the number of amendments in advance. Germaneness is also required once the Senate has invoked cloture, and those amendments must be submitted in advance of the cloture vote.

Senate Passage

Once all committee amendments and floor amendments have been completed, the bill is engrossed and read a third time. The question of passage is then put forth. Passage requires a simple majority. At any time prior to passage the bill may be laid on the table or postponed indefinitely which effectively kills the bill. Prior to passage the bill may also be made a special order for a day certain by a two-thirds majority vote; laid aside temporarily; recommitted to the original or another committee; or displaced by another bill by a majority vote.

Typically, bills are passed by voice vote. If there is a question, a division may be requested prior to the announced results of the voice vote. Before the results of either the voice vote or division, a roll call vote may be requested.

With a yea-and-nay vote, a senator who did not vote or who voted on the prevailing side may make a motion to reconsider the question. This motion must be made on the same calendar day or within the next two days of actual session. If the vote was by voice or division, any senator may make the motion to reconsider. The motion is usually tabled, which constitutes final determination. If the motion is agreed to, another vote on the question may be taken. If the motion is not agreed to, the first decision of the Senate is affirmed. A bill cannot be transmitted to the House if a motion to reconsider is left unresolved.

Transmittal to the House

Once the Senate finishes action on a bill, the official desk copy is endorsed as having been passed and sent to the secretary of the Senate and delivered to the bill clerk. The bill clerk turns it over to the enrolling clerk, who sends it to the Government Printing Office. The GPO prints the bill on special white paper in the form passed by the Senate. The bill, which is now technically an "Act of the Senate," becomes the official engrossed bill once attested to by the secretary of the Senate.

Engrossed bills, which may be original Senate bills or bills originally passed by the House and amended by the Senate, are transmitted to the House, and concurrence by the House is requested. The Speaker of the House may refer the bill to a committee or, if it is substantially similar to a previously House-passed measure, may keep the engrossed Senate bill on the Speaker's table, where it may be taken up or substituted for that of the similar House bill.

Resolving Differences Between the House and Senate

Senate bills returned to the Senate with House amendments are laid before the Senate. The House's amendments may be considered individually or en bloc. Any of the following motions are then in order: 1) a motion to refer to committee; 2) a motion to amend the amendments; 3) a motion to agree to the amendments; and 4) a motion to disagree and request a conference.

If the House amendments are referred to committee by the Senate, the committee may recommend amending the amendments, agreeing to the amendments or disagreeing to the amendments and requesting a conference. In fact, a conference may be requested at any stage during the consideration of amendments between the chambers.

If the House amendments are amended by the Senate, those Senate amendments are transmitted to the House with a request for concurrence. If the House agrees, legislative work on the bill is complete. The House may choose, however, to amend the Senate amendments to the House amendments. This is tantamount to a second-degree amendment and is therefore the last allowable amendment. These second-degree amendments would then be transmitted back to the Senate with a request for concurrence. If the Senate concurs, the process is complete. If the Senate disagrees to all or some of the second-degree House amendments, a conference will be requested.

Bills originating in the House will basically follow the same steps as above, but in reverse.

Conference Committee

The request for a conference can only be made by the chamber in possession of the bill's official papers. This has some significance, as the chamber asking for the conference typically acts last on the conference report, and a motion to recommit is not available to the chamber that acts last. As a result, you will occasionally see one chamber that expects the other will not concur vote to request a conference prior to returning the bill to the other chamber.

When the Senate requests a conference or agrees to the House's request for a conference, it names conferees and so instructs the House. The House takes much the same action. The House appoints conferees who may be instructed to accept or reject particular Senate amendments. These instructions are not binding to the conferees.

Conference members may be of any party but typically were very involved with the legislation as it moved through the legislative process. Each chamber may appoint as many conferees as they wish, but each chamber will have only one vote in the conference itself.

Once the conference is agreed to and conferees are named, all official papers on the measure are sent to the conference committee.

The conference committee has limited options and authority. The committee can deal only with matters in disagreement. They cannot insert new material or delete anything already agreed to by both chambers. There is more latitude, however, if the measure in conference is a bill that was passed in the nature of a substitute. In this case, both the original measure and the substitute is subject to conference, and a new third version may be reported. This new modified version must, of course, be germane.

After deliberations are completed, conferees can: 1) recommend that the House recede from all or certain amendments; 2) recommend that the Senate recede from its disagreement to all or certain House amendments (or vice versa); 3) recommend that the Senate recede from all or certain of its amendments or 4) recommend that the conference cannot agree.

If agreement cannot be reached by the conference, new conferees may be appointed in either or both chambers, and new instructions may be given.

Once agreement is reached, the conference committee reports back to each chamber. The report must be signed by a majority of each chamber's conferees. No minority views are printed. The engrossed bill, amendments, and one copy of the conference report are delivered to the chamber that will act first on the measure (the chamber that agreed to the conference requested by the other).

A conference report sent to the House must lie over three days before it can be considered, except during the last six days of session in which case it need only be made available to members two hours prior to consideration. In the Senate, a conference report may be brought up immediately. In either chamber, the conference report must be accepted or rejected in its entirety. The conference report is not subject to amendment.

Assuming the Senate acts first, the Senate may, prior to agreeing to the report, recommit it to the conferees by a majority vote. If the Senate votes to accept the report, the Senate conferees are discharged and the official papers with a message advising of the Senate action are delivered to the House.

The second chamber now acts on the conference report. A motion to recommit a conference report may not be made in the second chamber, as the conferees from the first chamber have already been discharged.

If the second chamber also agrees to the conference report, the bill is cleared for the president's signature. If some or all of the amendments are not agreed upon, another conference may be requested or the originating chamber may choose to recede from their amendments. Until all amendments in disagreement are reconciled, the bill cannot proceed to the president.

Enrollment

Once the two chambers reach agreement, the official papers are delivered to the enrolling clerk of the chamber in which the bill originated. The Government Printing Office prepares an enrolled version of the bill. Upon receipt of the enrolled version, either the secretary of the Senate or the clerk of the House endorses it. Assuming the bill is correct, the enrolling clerk attaches a slip stating that the bill has been examined and is correct. The enrolled bill is presented to the Speaker of the House for signature and then the vice president.

Once signed by the Speaker and vice president, the bill is transmitted to the president. If an error is discovered in the bill at this point, it can be corrected by a concurrent resolution asking that the bill be sent back for correction. If the error is discovered after enrollment but prior to delivery to the president, a concurrent resolution agreed to by both Houses can correct the error. If the bill is approved by the president with the error, only passage of another bill can correct the error.

Presidential Action

Once the enrolled bill is delivered to the president, the Constitution allows the President 10 days in which to act. If the president signs the bill, this information is transmitted to the appropriate chamber and the signed enrolled bill is delivered to the Archivist of the United States, who designates it either a public or private law and assigns it a number. An official copy is then sent to the GPO, who makes the slip law print.

The president may decide to veto the bill. If the president vetoes a bill it is returned to the House of origin with a statement of the president's objections, known as a veto message.

The president may also choose neither to sign the bill nor veto it during the allotted ten-day period. If this occurs while Congress is in session, the bill will become law. If the ten-day period extends beyond the date of final adjournment for Congress (sine die) and the president does not sign the bill, it fails to become law. This is known as a pocket veto.

Veto Override

Once a vetoed bill is returned to the originating chamber with the president's objections, it need not be voted on immediately. Consideration of the bill can be postponed, referred back to committee, or tabled. Once brought up, no fewer than two-thirds of the members must vote affirmatively to override the president's veto. If the originating House overrides the veto, the bill is transmitted to the second chamber where the process is repeated. If two-thirds or more of the second chamber also votes to override the veto the measure becomes law notwithstanding the objections of the president. If either chamber fails to reach the two-thirds threshold, the veto is sustained and the bill fails to become law.

House and Senate Gift Ban Rules

Both the House and Senate have stringent rules concerning what type and value of "gifts" members and staff can and cannot accept and from whom they can or cannot accept such gifts. Below is a synopsis of those rules. For complete details, refer to the actual House and Senate rules governing gifts.

Currently, the House rules are more stringent than the Senate rules. There has been, however, some discussion of bringing the House rules more in line with the Senate's gift rules.

In 1995 the House adopted Rule 52, which bans most gifts. This rule took effect January 1, 1996, and covers all members, officers, and employees of the House. The rule prohibits members, officers, and employees from accepting any gift, except as specifically provided by the rule. There is no longer a gift limit in the House. Effectively the limit is, no gifts, unless they come from relatives, personal friends or other members, officers, or employees of the House or Senate. Exceptions to the gift rule include personal hospitality; campaign contributions; contributions to legal expense funds; information materials; anything paid for by the federal, state, or local governments; opportunities available to the public at large; free attendance provided by the sponsor of a widely attended event; food or refreshment offered other than as a part of a meal; and items of nominal value such as T-shirts or caps.

The Senate rules are a bit less stringent. Rule XXXV of the Standing Rules of the Senate provides that no member, officer, or employee of the Senate shall accept a gift whose value which they reasonably believe to exceed $50.00 or a cumulative value of $100.00 from any one source during a calendar year. Gifts with a value less than $10.00 do not count towards the $100.00-per-year cumulative limit. The term "gift" is defined as any gratuity, favor, discount, entertainment, hospitality, loan, forbearance, or other item having monetary value. The term includes gifts of services, training, transportation, lodging, and meals, whether provided in kind, by purchase of a ticket, payment in advance, or reimbursement after the expense has been incurred. Gifts do not include campaign contributions; gifts from relatives; personal hospitality; anything paid for by federal, state, or local governments; contributions to legal expense funds; gifts from other members, officers, or employees of the House or Senate; free attendance at widely attended events; opportunities available to the public at large; food or refreshment of nominal value offered other than as part of a meal; T-shirts and caps; and certain specified food, refreshment, and lodging benefits offered in connection with their official duties.

Additional Resources

For more information on Congressional procedures, refer to the following publications:

- *House Rules and Manual: Constitution, Jefferson's Manual, and Rules of the House of Representatives of the United States,* prepared by Charles W. Johnson, Parliamentarian of the House.

- *Deschler-Brown Precedents of the United States House of Representatives,* by Lewis Deschler, Parliamentarian of the House (1928–1974), Wm. Holmes Brown, Parliamentarian of the House (1974–1994).

- *House Practice: A Guide to the Rules, Precedents and Procedures of the House,* by Wm. Holmes Brown, Parliamentarian of the House (1974–1994)

- *Senate Procedure,* by Floyd M. Riddick, Parliamentarian Emeritus of the Senate, and Alan S. Frumin, Parliamentarian of the Senate.

CHAPTER 17

The Federal Budget and Appropriations Process

Michael E. Kastner

THE CONSTITUTION provides Congress the authority to put in place rules to create a federal budget. The primary purpose of the budget is to provide a measure of federal expenditures and then to provide a means to collect and allocate the resources necessary for those expenditures.

The budget process often is thought of as complex and arcane. At its simplest, the budget process can be broken down into only a few parts. First, Congress must authorize the expenditure of funds. Second, Congress must appropriate those funds. And finally, Congress must raise those funds.

Recent History

In 1974, Congress passed the Congressional Budget and Impoundment Act (commonly known as the Budget Act of 1974). This act was written to better coordinate the federal budgeting process. (Before 1974 there was no framework within which Congress could establish its spending and revenue priorities.) The Budget Act also was a response to what Congress perceived as budgetary abuses by the president.

The Budget Act created the House and Senate Budget Committees, which oversee the budget process, and the Congressional Budget Office (CBO), which serves as the official scorekeeper for the budget.

The President's Budget

In the first major step in the budget process, the president submits a budget to Congress. The president is required to submit a budget request for the upcoming fiscal year to Congress on the first Monday in February. The administration typically begins preparing this request 18 months before the start of the applicable fiscal year.

The president's budget request submission was codified by the Budget and Accounting Act of 1921. This act also created the General Accounting Office (GAO), which is the government's auditing body and is responsible solely to Congress. Additionally, the act created the Bureau of the Budget (later renamed the Office of Management and Budget [OMB]), which oversees the executive branch's role in the budget process.

Michael E. Kastner

The Congressional Budget Resolution

The Congressional Budget Resolution is a concurrent resolution that allows Congress to put in place a framework within which it will consider separate spending, taxing, and debt-limiting measures. As a concurrent resolution, it is not public law and does not need to be signed by the president but only approved by both chambers of the Congress. A budget resolution is not legally binding. A budget resolution may not be filibustered. The budget resolution also starts the reconciliation process, which conforms current revenue and spending laws to congressional budget policies.

Once the president has submitted a budget request, the Senate and House Budget Committees begin debate, holding hearings, and receiving testimony. Other committees also submit their views on portions of the budget to the Budget Committees. Committee views are to be received within six weeks of the president's budget request submission.

By April 1, the Senate Budget Committee is to report a resolution, and by April 15 Congress is to complete the resolution. In fact, final agreement often is not reached until months after the April 15 deadline. The Budget Act prohibits consideration of revenue, spending, and debt-limit measures until the budget resolution has been adopted, but exceptions are provided. The House is allowed to consider regular appropriations bills after May 15 even without a budget resolution.

The budget resolution should set aggregate budget levels for the next fiscal year and planning levels for the following four fiscal years.

In recent years Congress has used special authority to extend the budget resolution beyond five years.

Section 301 of the Budget Act sets out the budget resolution's components. The components are budget totals, spending broken down by budget function, reconciliation instructions, budget enforcement mechanisms, and statements of policy.

Budget totals set targets for total revenues, total spending, and the resultant budget deficit or surplus. Budget totals are provided as budget aggregates or committee allocations. Budget aggregates are total revenues, total new budget authority, total outlays, and revenues and Social Security outlays.

Floor consideration of the budget resolution is guided by the rules of the chamber. In the House, the Rules Committee typically reports a special rule establishing the terms and conditions under which the budget resolution will be debated. The Senate generally relies more heavily on agreements reached by the leadership (see section on unanimous consent agreements in Chapter 16 on Congressional Procedures).

Reconciliation

When the Budget Act was first written, it included a process known as reconciliation. Reconciliation was originally intended as a method by which Congress could fine-tune revenue and spending levels at the end of the year without worry of a filibuster. Reconciliation is an optional practice but one that has been used widely in recent years and for reasons not necessarily originally envisioned.

Reconciliation has become a vehicle for implementing major economic change. Reconciliation instructions are now critical components of a budget resolution.

The reconciliation process has two stages: first, the adoption of reconciliation instructions in the budget resolution; and second, the enactment of reconciliation legislation to change revenue or spending laws.

Budget resolution instructions direct committees to change existing law by a specified amount but do leave to the committee how theses changes should be made. The instructions usually specify a deadline for the changes.

The legislative changes dictated by the reconciliation instructions usually are consolidated by the budget committees into an omnibus bill, but are not substantively changed by the committees. If leadership does deem changes necessary, they usually draft floor amendments. The Budget Act requires that any such amendments be deficit neutral. Nongermane amendments are prohibited in both chambers.

The Byrd Rule

In 1985 the Senate adopted the Byrd Rule, and it became a permanent part of the Budget Act in 1990. The Byrd Rule allows a senator to raise a point of order against extraneous material in a reconciliation bill. A motion to waive this point of order requires an affirmative three-fifths vote. The Byrd Rule applies to the reconciliation bill and any amendments or conference report associated with it.

Under the Byrd Rule, an amendment or provision is extraneous if it produces no change in outlays or revenues, increases outlays, or reduces revenues, and the reporting committee fails to achieve its instructed dollar change, is not within the jurisdiction of the committee reporting the title, produces changes in outlays or revenues that are "merely incidental" to the nonbudgetary components of the provision, increases the deficit in any year beyond the years reconciled and such increase is not offset by other provisions in the same title, or provides certain changes in the Social Security program.

Budget Resolution Enforcement and Section 302

Budget resolution policies are implemented through enactment of annual appropriations bills, revenue measures, debt-limit legislation, and reconciliation bills. To better enforce the budget resolution, Congress relies on the committee system.

The Budget committees allocate the budget resolution's spending amounts among House and Senate committees. Committee allocation is the means by which budget resolution spending totals are turned into budget authority and outlays for committee action on spending bills. Committee allocations also are referred to as section 302 (or section 602 for fiscal years 1991–1998) allocations.

Section 302 (602 for fiscal years 1991–1998) creates a two-step allocation procedure. First, the spending totals for the fiscal year are distributed to committees. Second, each committee suballocates the spending totals among its subcommittees or programs. The amounts of new budget authority (the authority permitting government agencies to enter into financial obligations) and outlays (actual disbursements by the Federal Treasury) allocated to the committees must not exceed the aggregate amount of budget authority and outlays set forth by the budget resolution.

The Budget Act provides both substantive and procedural points of order to block violations of the budget resolution. During floor debate, the Budget Committee chairs typically state whether or not a particular measure violates one of these points of order. If no point of order is raised, or the point of order is waived, the violating measure may be considered.

In addition to congressional discretionary spending caps included in the budget resolution, there also are statutory spending caps that are enforced through sequestration.

Discretionary and Mandatory Spending

Mandatory (or direct) spending refers to programs whose spending level is governed by formulas or criteria set forth in the authorizing legislation as opposed to an appropriations bill. Examples of mandatory spending programs include Social Security, Medicare, veterans' pensions, and interest payments on the public debt. Mandatory spending often is referred to as entitlement spending. Entitlement spending is actually a subset of mandatory spending, albeit the largest such subset.

Discretionary spending refers to spending that is not mandatory. Discretionary spending is subject to annual funding decisions in the appropriations process. Most federal government operations are funded through discretionary spending. Examples of discretionary spending include funding for the Department of Defense, the Internal Revenue Service, and the Environmental Protection Agency.

Discretionary spending is implemented through the annual appropriations acts. Mandatory, or direct, spending usually is implemented through other substantive legislation.

Sequestration and PAYGO

The Gramm-Rudman-Hollings Act of 1985 set annual deficit targets and created an automatic spending reduction process known as sequestration. The Budget Enforcement Act (BEA) of 1990 further amended this process and provides that if OMB estimates that an appropriations bill will result in an excess of statutorily set discretionary spending limits, then the president must issue a sequester order. The sequester order reduces all nonexempt discretionary accounts by a uniform percentage. A few specified discretionary programs are exempt or fall under special rules in the event of a sequester.

BEA also created two enforcement processes known as pay-as-you-go, or PAYGO, for mandatory spending. One PAYGO is a congressional mechanism, and the other is a statutory one. BEA created a point of order, requiring a three-fifths vote to waive, against consideration of any legislation that would increase the deficit over the next ten years. The result is that Congress must pay for any program changes. This order applies to all legislation other than appropriations bills (to which apply other enforcement mechanisms). These PAYGO violations are determined by CBO, and the rule is scheduled to sunset at the end of fiscal year 2002.

BEA requires OMB to enforce PAYGO for direct spending and revenues. The executive branch PAYGO has the same effect as a point of order; Congress is required to pay for any changes or risk a sequester. Unlike discretionary spending, however, most direct spending is either exempt or subject to special rules under a sequester.

Appropriations

Appropriations are acts of Congress that permit federal agencies to incur obligations and make payments for specified purposes. Appropriations are the most common method of providing budget authority. The power of appropriation is derived from the Constitution and is exclusively legislative in nature.

Congress passes three types of appropriations: regular, supplemental, and continuing. Regular appropriations provide budget authority to agencies for the next fiscal year. Supplemental appropriations provide additional budget authority during a current fiscal year. Continuing appropriations provide stop-gap funding for an agency that has not received its regular appropriation before the start of the fiscal year.

There are currently thirteen regular appropriations bills each year that correspond with the thirteen appropriations subcommittees. By precedent, appropriations originate in the House. The House subcommittees are guided by the discretionary spending limits established under the section 302 (or 602) allocations. The Senate typically considers appropriations measures after they have been passed by the House.

In addition to providing funding, appropriations measures often place substantive limitations on federal agencies, even though legislating (authorizing) on an appropriations bill is technically prohibited. Limitations may restrict the way in which appropriated funds are used. For example, an appropriations bill may forbid an agency from using any of its funds to promulgate rules on a specified issue. These limiting amendments often are used to bring major policy issues to a vote.

The standard appropriation is for a single fiscal year. In some cases, Congress will make multiyear appropriations that make funds available for specified periods of two or more fiscal years. Congress also can make no-year appropriations, where funds remain available until expended.

Revenue Legislation

The Constitution vests Congress with the power to levy taxes. The Constitution stipulates that all revenue measures originate in the House. Such revenue measures fall under the jurisdiction of the Ways and Means Committee. In rare instances, the Senate will take the initiative on revenue measures by attaching them to a previously House-passed revenue measure. This method does pass constitutional muster but is not likely to be well regarded by the House.

Congress generally acts on revenue measures within the context of the budget, as the revenue totals of the budget dictate subsequent action on revenue measures. Because the budget resolution only specifies revenue totals, the actual means for raising those revenues are determined by committees with appropriate jurisdiction.

Debt Limit Legislation

Federal borrowing is subject to a debt limit, which is statutorily set. While operating in a deficit mode, this limit occasionally must be raised. This legislation falls under the jurisdiction of the House Ways and Means Committee and the Senate Finance Committee.

Impoundments, Rescissions, and Deferrals

An impoundment is an action or inaction by an officer or employee of the U.S. government that delays or withholds the obligation or expenditure of budget authority provided by law. This action is considered a deviation from the intention of Congress.

There are two categories of impoundments: rescissions and deferrals. Rescissions are the cancellation of budget authority before the time such authority would expire. Deferrals delay the obligation of budget authority beyond the point it would normally occur.

Rescissions are proposed by the president in a message to Congress. The message sets forth the amount, the program, and the reason for the rescission. Congress has forty-five days of continuous session during which it can pass the rescission. If Congress does not pass the rescission, the president must make the funds available for obligation and expenditure.

Deferrals are proposed by the president in a message similar to a rescission message to Congress. The president may not propose deferrals that extend beyond the end of the fiscal year in which the proposed deferral is made. Congress may overturn a deferral by passing a law that disapproves the deferral.

Line Item Veto

The 104th Congress passed the Line Item Veto Act, which empowers the president to veto individual items of appropriation. In addition to annual appropriations, the line item veto power also applies to new entitlement spending and targeted tax benefits.

The president has five days after he signs an act into law within which to send a line item veto message to Congress. Upon receipt of the message in Congress, the spending is considered canceled. The savings are placed in a "lockbox" to prevent them from being spent elsewhere. All line item veto savings go toward deficit reduction. The only ways to cancel spending and not have the savings go to deficit reduction would be for the president to veto the entire piece of legislation or make use of the rescission or deferral.

Congress has a limited time within which it can introduce disapproval legislation to overturn the president's cancellation. Once disapproval legislation has passed both chambers in identical form, it is enrolled and presented to the president. If the president signs the disapproval legislation, the cancellations are nullified and become effective on the effective date of the original legislation. If the president vetoes the disapproval legislation, the cancellations remain in effect unless two-thirds of each chamber vote to override the veto.

Unfunded Mandates

In 1995, Congress passed the Unfunded Mandates Reform Act (UMRA). This act separates mandates imposed on the private sector from intergovernmental mandates. Intergovernmental mandates are those imposed on state, local, and tribal governments.

The intent of UMRA was to make it difficult for the federal government to force expensive new programs that do not pay for themselves on the private sector or nonfederal governments. UMRA requires that the CBO estimate the costs of bills with federal mandates reported out of committees. Private-sector mandates must be identified if they will have a direct cost equal to or greater than $100 million in any of the first five fiscal years for which it is effective. The threshold for intergovernmental mandates is $50 million.

UMRA does not apply to existing mandates. UMRA exempts unfunded mandates that enforce the constitutional rights of individuals or prohibit discrimination based on race, sex, age, or disability. The president or Congress also can designate legislation as an "emergency" measure, which exempts it from UMRA provisions.

The act allows a point of order in both the House and Senate against any bill or joint resolution reported by an authorizing committee that does not have a CBO statement or would result in mandates exceeding the $50 million or $100 million limits. A bill is considered to be in order if it provides funding to cover the new costs imposed by the mandate. A simple majority vote is needed to override such a point of order.

UMRA also requires federal agencies to assess the effects of new mandates and to minimize the financial impact whenever possible.

Budget and Appropriations Timetable

Date	Action
5 days before president's budget submission	CBO sequester preview report.
1st Monday in February	President's budget submission (includes OMB sequester and adjustments to spending caps).
Within 6 weeks of president's budget	Committees submit views and estimates to the Budget Committees.
April 1	Senate Budget Committee reports budget resolution.
April 15	Congress completes budget resolution. If not, chair of House Budget Committee files 302(a) allocations; Ways and Means is free to proceed with pay-as-you-go measures.
May 15	Appropriations bills may be considered in the House.
June 10	House Appropriations reports last bill.
End of previous session to June 30	If an appropriations bill violates caps, OMB sequesters 15 days after enactment.
June 30	House completes action on annual appropriations bills.
July 15	President submits mid-session review.
August 10	President's notification on military personnel exemption.
August 15	CBO sequester update report.
August 20	OMB sequester update report.
October 1	Fiscal year begins.
10 days after end of session	CBO final sequester report.
15 days after end of session	OMB final sequester report.
45 days after end of session	GAO compliance report.

Andrew C. Briscoe III has been Director of Public Policy since 1994 at the Salt Institute, an Alexandria, Virginia-based international trade association representing companies producing salt. The Institute advocates salt industry policy on such issues as human health, highway traffic safety, water conditioning, and worker safety. Previously, he directed the successful federal and state public affairs and public policy initiatives of Mothers Against Drunk Driving, working with transportation allies including the Department of Transportation, the National Highway Traffic Safety Administration, Congress, the Bush administration, the U.S. Supreme Court, and the National Commission on Drunk Driving. He currently serves on the ASAE Government Relations Section Council.

Michelle K. Brooks presently works for the Manufactured Housing Institute (MHI) in Washington, D.C., in the field of government affairs. Prior to joining MHI, she was the Regional Director for Political Affairs with the Western Mobilehome Parkowners Association, overseeing lobbying activities in nearly 100 communities. She has eighteen years of political experience, including work in campaign operations and fundraising and as a staff assistant to a member of the California State Legislature.

Dennis Brown, CAE, joined the Equipment Leasing Association (ELA) in 1993 as Director of State Government Relations to implement a proactive state government relations program. His responsibilities include legislative and regulatory issues in all 50 states. Former Vice-Chairman of the ASAE Government Relations Section Council, he is the 1998–99 president of the State Government Affairs Council.

John Chwat is president of Chwat and Company, Inc., a government relations firm based in Alexandria, Virginia, that represents trade and professional associations, corporations, and business interests in federal and state public affairs. Since 1971 his work has included serving as chief of staff to two members of Congress, as well as with a Senate committee staff, the Congressional Affairs Office of the U.S. Department of Agriculture, Congressional Research Service, and COMSAT Corp., and, since 1980, in the private sector representing his own clients. He is a member of the ASAE Government Relations Section and for many years has coordinated ASAE Roundtables and other programs in the government relations area.

William A. Franco serves as Deputy Director, State Advocacy, at the American Association of Health Plans (AAHP) in Washington, D.C. AAHP represents more than 1,000 health maintenance organizations, preferred provider organizations, and similar network-based plans. Prior to joining AAHP, he served for six years as Director of Government Affairs at the Pharmaceutical Care Management Association in Arlington, Virginia. He also served four years as a Special Assistant to the Director, United States Information Agency during the Reagan and Bush Administrations and five years as Legislative Assistant to Congressman Daniel E. Lungren (R-CA). He currently serves on the ASAE Government Relations Section Council.

Charlotte Herbert is Vice President of Government Affairs for Associated Builders and Contractors (ABC) and is responsible for the day-to-day operations of the legislative, regulatory, legal, and political development departments. She serves as ABC's lead lobbyist, is active in numerous congressional leadership and member roundtables, and serves on the steering committees of many industry coalitions. She manages the association's political action committee and political education fund. She serves on the ASAE Government Affairs Section Council and is currently chair of the Roundtables Committee.

Michael E. Kastner directs the Washington office of the Michigan-based National Truck Equipment Association (NTEA) and serves as treasurer for the association's political action committee. In 1995 this government relations program won an ASAE Government Relations Award of Excellence. He currently serves on ASAE's Public Policy Committee and is a past chairman of both the School of Association Government Relations and the Government Relations Roundtables Committee. Prior to becoming the NTEA's first director of government relations, he held state relations positions with Lear Siegler, Inc., and the Motor Vehicle Manufacturers Association.

Marcie M. McNelis, CAE, has been a principal in MultiState Associates, Inc., a fifty-state and local government relations firm providing lobbying, monitoring, and issue-tracking services to associations and corporations since 1990. She spent seventeen years in association management, including thirteen years as executive director of the State Government Affairs Council. She was the 1995–96 chair of the ASAE Government Relations Section Council, and is currently a member of the Executive Committee of the Center for Advocacy and Government Ethics under the National Conference of State Legislatures Foundation for State Legislatures.

E. Colette Nelson is Executive Vice President of the American Subcontractors Association, Inc. (ASA) in Alexandria, Virginia, a national association representing more than 6,000 subcontractors in all the construction trades. During her 15 years with ASA, she has been actively involved in most of the major issues facing the construction industry, including small business development, government procurement, labor-management relations, and taxes. She is also immediate past chair of the Government Relations Section Council of the American Society of Association Executives and an *ex officio* member of ASAE's Board of Directors. She also serves as secretary of the Small Business Legislative Council, a federation of 100 small business groups.

Michael P. O'Brien, CAE, is Assistant Staff Vice President, State and Local Affiliate Services, with the National Association of Home Builders (NAHB), overseeing the activities and departments that serve its 880 affiliates and chapters. He also oversees NAHB's Labor, Safety and Health Services Department, which is responsible for regulatory lobbying, seminars, and educational materials on occupational safety and health and employment issues. Prior to joining NAHB in 1989, he served as assistant director of government relations for the American Subcontractors Association. He is a member of the ASAE Government Relations Section Council.

Brian Pallasch, CAE, is currently Director of Government Relations at the American Subcontractors Association (ASA), in Alexandria, Virginia. Having been with ASA since 1996, he is responsible for all federal and state relations at ASA. He currently serves as Chairman of the Procurement Committee of the Small Business Legislative Council and as a member of Regulatory Affairs Committee of the U.S. Chamber of Commerce. Prior to joining ASA, Pallasch served as the Director of Government Relations for the American Society of Association Executives.

Pamela Phillips presently serves as Vice-President of Government Relations for the American Chiropractic Association (ACA). In addition, she spearheads lobbying efforts directed at Capitol Hill, the White House, and appropriate regulatory agencies. She previously served as Senior Lobbyist, Associate Director of Government Affairs, and Associate Director of State Relations for the American Physical Therapy Association and has over seventeen years of experience in the government relations field.

John M. Sharbaugh, CAE, is Vice President of State Societies and Regulatory Affairs for the American Institute of Certified Public Accountants (AICPA). In this position, he has primary responsibility for relations with state CPA societies and coordinates the institute's efforts on federal and state regulatory issues. He oversees the AICPA's State Legislation Department, Federal Key Person Program, Congressional Luncheon Program, and Member Roundtable Program. He is currently vice chair of the ASAE Government Relations Section Council and also serves as co-chair of the Professional Liability Task Force of the American Tort Reform Association.

Aaron K. Trippler is Director of Government Affairs for the American Industrial Hygiene Association (AIHA), directing government affairs for more than 70 local sections and acting as chief liaison with Congress and federal agencies. Prior to his affiliation with AIHA, he served as Executive Director of Health Care Solutions for America and as Vice President for Communicating for Agriculture, both national nonprofit organizations. He has also served as Chief of Staff to the Senate IR Caucus of the Minnesota State Senate.